Fifteen Things They Forgot
to Tell You About Autism

of related interest

Coming Home to Autism
A Room-by-Room Approach to Supporting Your
Child at Home after ASD Diagnosis
Tara Leniston and Rhian Grounds
ISBN 978 1 78592 436 1
eISBN 978 1 78450 808 1

Talking with Your Child about Their Autism Diagnosis
A Guide for Parents
Raelene Dundon
ISBN 978 1 78592 277 0
eISBN 978 1 78450 577 6

The Parents' Practical Guide to Resilience for
Children aged 2–10 on the Autism Spectrum
Jeanette Purkis and Emma Goodall
ISBN 978 1 78592 274 9
eISBN 978 1 78450 574 5

A Parents' ABC of the Autism Spectrum
Stephen Heydt
ISBN 978 1 78592 164 3
eISBN 978 1 78450 435 9

15 Things They Forgot to Tell You About Autism

The Stuff That Transformed My Life as an Autism Parent

Debby Elley

Jessica Kingsley *Publishers*
London and Philadelphia

First published in 2018
by Jessica Kingsley Publishers
73 Collier Street
London N1 9BE, UK
and
400 Market Street, Suite 400
Philadelphia, PA 19106, USA

www.jkp.com

Library of Congress Cataloging in Publication Data
Names: Elley, Debby, author.
Title: Fifteen things they forgot to tell you about autism : the stuff that
   transformed my life as an autism parent / Debby Elley.
Description: London ; Philadelphia : Jessica Kingsley Publishers, [2018]
Identifiers: LCCN 2017058450 | ISBN 9781785924385 (alk. paper)
Subjects: LCSH: Autism in children. | Parents of autistic children.
Classification: LCC RJ506.A9 E4435 2018 | DDC 618.92/85882--
dc23 LC record available at https://lccn.loc.gov/2017058450

British Library Cataloguing in Publication Data
A CIP catalogue record for this book is available from the British Library

ISBN 978 1 78592 438 5
eISBN 978 1 78450 810 4

Printed and bound in the United States

· · · · · · · · · · · · · ·

This book is dedicated to Alec and Bobby. The two of you are amazing kids, and I'm one lucky mum. Alec, if I had to put up with daily confusion and overload, I'm not sure I'd do it with a dazzling smile on my face the way you do. Bobby, you are one brave guy, you've faced your fears and have made us really proud. You two inspire all that I do.

I'd also like to dedicate this book to the nurse (an actual nurse) who recently responded to the news I had twins with autism by saying, 'JESUS – BOTH?!' Just to let you know that difference is not a disaster, love.

· · · · · · · · · · · · · ·

Contents

Acknowledgements

Thanks to my patient husband, Gavin, who has never demanded that I get a 'proper' job and has enabled me to spend my days dreaming up funny headlines and new ways of explaining autism when it's been far from lucrative. Thanks to Tori Houghton, my partner in crime at *AuKids*, who is the best fun to be around and who created the concept of the Autism Sundae Dessert with me. Thanks to my family, my mum, dad and brothers, who all had their place in creating a positive thinker of me. High fives to my friends, particularly Emma, Vanessa, Kath and Alison for their enthusiasm for this project. Special thanks to teachers M'lanie Seton, Trish Larkin, Gareth Morewood, Stella Parkin, Jill Hallas and Phil Kerr.

I'd also like to thank the rest of the team who have given their time and dedication to our social enterprise *AuKids*. They've made it possible for Tori and I to share our positive ideas and for me to continue doing so with this book. They are graphic designer Jo 'Very Patient' Perry of Periscope

Studios, our autism advocate Tim 'Flex' Tuff, Paul Clare at R&P Printers, photographer David Laslett (who is also chief Cat Advisor) and Andy Davies of Fins Design and Print, who produces the *AuKids* clothing range and donates a percentage of the takings to our social enterprise.

I'd also like to thank our *AuKids* readers for their loyalty and their faith in our positive messages.

Finally, thanks to Ernie the cat who sat on my laptop case.

Notes on the Text

The random quotes at the start of each chapter are what I call 'Bobbyisms'. They are taken from my Facebook posts and have become quite popular, so I thought I'd share some with you.

I tend to use a lot of phrases and idioms. If you're reading this and you are autistic, ironically you may find this book a pain in the backside. For those for whom English isn't a first language and for people with autism, the most unusual phrases are listed and explained at the back of this book, but do keep an interpreter handy.

Introduction

Please don't do what I do and skip the introduction. Once you've read the introduction, you might decide that you don't want to read the rest of the book. So really, it will save you time. I'd recommend it.

Let's start with the big question. Why am I being arrogant enough to assume that the world could do with another book on autism?

Since my twins were diagnosed with autism in 2006, there's been a veritable explosion of autism books on the market. I am extremely glad that there is now such a lot of help out there. As co-editor of *AuKids*, an (ahem, award-winning) autism parenting magazine, I read, review and recommend plenty of them.

One thing I don't come across often enough, though, is books written by parents.

Parents are on the inside and outside of autism at the same time. They speak both languages – what I call English and Aut-speak. So, they have something special to share with the rest of the world.

When I write about my own experiences of autism, our readers say it gives them a sense of connection, a feeling of being included. As an autism parent, there's nothing to match that 'Oh, that happens to ME!' feeling.

Autism parenting is a club like no other, with rewards and challenges like no others. Going it alone shouldn't be an option when there's a world of people out there in the same boat. Some of them will even be rowing in the right direction.

It's not just my personal experiences of autism I want to share (who cares – you have your own life), but the insight into my twins, Bobby and Alec, that I've gained through ten years of writing and researching for the UK's first autism parenting magazine.

It's now been over a decade since Bobby and Alec received their autism diagnoses. Eleven years of learning, making mistakes and being surrounded by fascinating people who know more than I do. Wouldn't it be great if I could condense that learning into a book – a whizzy-whizz guide so that you don't have to be ten years older and wiser before you learn what I did?

As I write these pages, I know for sure that I'm not reflecting purely on my own experience of autism. My professional insight tells me that my own life is way more familiar to other families than you might suppose.

I wanted to put into words how I've watched my twin sons emerge from their shells over the last ten years, sharing the ways that I helped to make that happen without going stark, raving bonkers.

This isn't an autobiography. It's a parent's-eye view of autism, not explored through a textbook or clinical terminology but through the real-life experiences of its author.

So, there you go, you get both parent and professional: two for the price of one. Personal experiences, professional insights – hopefully learning and laughter combined. That's the idea anyhow. That's sort of what I promised the publisher.

At this juncture, I feel I should point out that I'm not in any way a Super Parent, if they exist. I simply believe that if you do some good stuff enough of the time, it works. The rest of the time, you can chat to your friends, watch undemanding TV or simply lie on the sofa going, 'Ugg. I should get up really. But I'm sooo tired.'

In fact, you should be timetabling in these things, because every autism parent knows that recharging is a must. This is a long-haul flight and you're the captain, first officer, stewardess and the bloke on the runway waving table-tennis bats.

As we shuffle along the next pages together, let me be your guide and your interpreter through the complex world of Real-Life Autism. At times, I'll be as lost as you. But fear not, I have my trusty sword of humour to axe through the awful jargon and historic mythology that surround the spectrum. As we wade through the traditional definitions and the assumptions that people make about autistic kids, let's put the world to rights, tell it how it really is, with love, warmth and laughter.

I've chosen 15 things to tell you that I wish it hadn't taken me so long to learn. They're not all about autism

– we start with your own state of mind and what it takes to approach your travels unblinkered. I'll share with you a positive mindset I have learnt that has helped me to view challenges head on and without despair. The more you think like this, the easier it becomes.

Later, it comes down to the nitty gritty of autism – 'stuff' that we all face day in, day out, like adapting to another person's way of thinking, helping them to interact with you, respecting survival defences while helping your child to adapt to a world that wasn't purpose-built for autism. My 'lightbulb' moments sometimes came because I had a strong network of experienced professionals around me. Not everyone does, so at least through this book I can give you that advantage.

Autism is complex and autism is confusing. But living with autism has made me a better person and it's taught me what real life should be about.

That's the intense bit. It's true but it's sort of worthy at the same time.

So, come on, what are you waiting for? We'll travel together to the first chapter…

Oh, wait. Have we time to stop for a coffee first?

1 Autism Is a Pick 'n' Mix

Personalise your autism learning

Age seven, Bobby's summary for his end-of-year report: 'In Year One I have become the ultimate champion of everything.'

When I started thinking about this book, Bobby was 11 and Alec was 11, too. That's right, they're twins. I have twins on the autism spectrum.

But a bit like the famous song about Scotland, one took the High Road and one took the Low Road. Bobby is, for want of a better expression, 'high functioning' (I'll explain why I hate that phrase later) and Alec has developed at a very different rate, has learning difficulties and is non-verbal, so he is taking a more picturesque route towards independence.

A bit of context

Alec's learning difficulties were caused by a near-fatal brain injury he sustained when he was almost two years old. One early September morning, I was brushing my teeth in the bathroom when he crawled on to the windowsill of his bedroom and squeezed himself, with what I imagine was some difficulty, through the small space between the criss-cross bars of his window.

He fell on to the patio 15 feet below. I say it quickly to get it over with, and because I don't mean to make you gasp, but everyone does when they hear this.

I was later told that a child who didn't have autism would not have selected this window as a challenge. An innate sense of fear would have kicked in. We didn't know he had autism and we certainly didn't know how determined he would be to override our safety measures. That very determination, however, helped him survive what happened next.

Alec was in a medically induced coma for 72 hours and when he awoke, the slate had been wiped clean. He couldn't lift his head, let alone sit up. The small amount of words he had were lost and haven't yet returned.

He had sustained a life-changing brain injury and it took him over a year to learn to walk again. But walk he did, against some predictions, and then he ran and then he learnt to swim (in a kind of upright pedalling style that British Olympic medallist Tom Daley has yet to recognise as an official stroke) and he can cycle a three-wheeler, too.

From the day of his accident on, we were simply grateful for Alec's survival. When you think someone could have died, their every living moment is a celebration.

The reason I have summarised what happened to Alec with such alarming brevity is for the benefit of context. Maybe it will help you to understand why nothing that has happened since has ever really been a big deal to us.

In big-deal terms, that capped it all.

So, this new label that our twins were branded with the following year – 'autism' – was a deal, certainly. A concern? Of course. A big deal? No.

Maybe we had no energy left to worry.

Autism is something that our twins were born with, so when they were diagnosed with it a year after Alec's accident, perhaps we accepted it easier and sooner than other people might have done.

It was part of who they were, very different from an accident.

Because of this, our perspective on autism has been accepting from the start. Other parents might have been expecting a 'perfect' child only to be told that they were 'lacking' in some way.

To us, however, when faced with the conundrum about whether we'd end up with a child at all, or one with autism, we took the latter option quite gratefully. We nearly lost Alec altogether. I can't underestimate how much of a perspective this gave us on his autism.

Not that we had a clue what autism was.

I thought I knew what autism was. Autism meant lousy with people, right?

We parents can be very judgemental when faced with ignorance (I'm the worst in this respect), but flick back a few pages in your own life story and there was a point when Dustin Hoffman in *Rain Man* was the start and end of your knowledge, too.

Looking back, with the benefit of hindsight, our twins were showing clear signs of autism from early babyhood, I just hadn't known enough to pick up on it.

When faced with anything that had wheels, Alec used to upend it and spin them. In fact, when faced with pretty much anything, Alec would spin it. I remember being quite impressed as he spun a cube on its corner.

Bobby would kneel with his legs making a characteristic 'w' shape, which on its own wasn't a sign but combined with the flapping and humming, it was pretty much a neon light.

It didn't occur to me that this might be autism, because they laughed and giggled. Dustin Hoffman's character did neither.

When we were finally told they had autism in November 2006, I remember sensing a void in my brain where information should have been. That terrible powerless feeling was what drove me so hard to learn so much so quickly – and I'm not on my own.

Parents, in my experience, either completely bury their heads in the sand (ostriches) or delve into books and pamphlets immediately (owls). It's only just this minute occurred to me how useful being an owl would have been as they were growing up, what with the rotating head, nocturnal lifestyle and all that.

The fact I had to wade through so much codswallop (for our overseas readers, codswallop is an English term meaning 'utter rubbish') to get to the good information was partly what inspired my friend Tori Houghton and myself to launch a magazine two years later. Essentially, to trudge through the rubbish and summarise it so that other parents wouldn't have to. Strangely enough, 'wading through codswallop so that you don't have to' has never been our tagline. Missed a trick there.

Anyway, autism was here and it was here to stay.

The way that you live with 'different' sometimes has a lot to do with the very earliest messages you receive about autism. If it's presented to you in a doom-and-gloom fashion, you will take it from the professionals that this news is indeed doom-and-gloom worthy.

If, however, it's presented to you in a 'No problem, you'll sail through this one!' sort of way, that is quite obviously a Big Lie designed to set you up for disappointment and failure.

Most practitioners decide to tread the middle line but, unfortunately, they are scuppered by some unfortunate traditions and terminology.

First, the problem of tradition. Because diagnosis takes place in a hospital or specialist clinic, autism is presented to parents in the same way as any medical diagnosis would be.

Thus, we parents are primed for the bad news that something is horribly WRONG with our child and indeed even the word 'diagnosis' confirms that terrible conclusion. Incidentally, autism researcher and lecturer Dr Luke Beardon argues against using the word 'diagnosis' for this very reason.

Our second difficulty comes with the common terminology used to explain autism. Autism is a neurological collection of traits, some helpful and some not so helpful.

To recognise these traits collectively, the term 'Triad of Impairments' was introduced many years ago and has only recently been replaced. Even though our understanding of autism has improved dramatically, the Triad terminology still looms large.

When my twins were diagnosed in 2006, the Triad of Impairments was the first description of autism that I received.

Me: 'Hello autism, who are you?'

Autism (booming voice): 'I am The Triad of Impairments.'

Me: (Run a mile.)

You will be wondering what the Triad of Impairments are, so here goes. Your child is impaired in the areas of communication, social interaction and imagination. Sensory issues have been bolted on for good measure recently. And that's it. There's your autism. See you soon, bye-bye parents.

You'll be thinking by now, 'Noooo, she's exaggerating! Surely there is more explanation than that?'

Unless you are an autism parent, and then you'll know I'm not exaggerating.

The definition, when it was first used, was a groundbreaking way of defining the core traits of autism. These days, it is the simplicity itself that causes parents to be bewildered, as what lies behind each core trait isn't usually adequately explained.

How much information you get depends on the part of the country (or even which country) we are talking about. But I'm afraid a lot of us are left at the mercy of the internet, a scary place where fact and fiction aren't easy to decipher from one another.

Although the term 'Triad of Impairments' lingers, in 2013 an updated description of autism was announced. While it carries more detail (which I'll go into later), there's still a difficulty in translating clinical terminology into useable, positive information for parents.

I went home and imagined both my boys rocking to themselves (in parkas for some inexplicable reason – but these days they do look a bit like the Gallagher brothers from Oasis so maybe that was just a premonition), unable to talk to anybody, make friends or get married.

Then I went into their bedroom and saw their cheerful grins and that vision didn't quite seem right. So, I decided to learn a bit more, to understand why there was such a drastic mismatch between my simple understanding of what it meant to have autism and the giggly, funny, loving boys who greeted me from their cots each morning.

'Triad of Impairments'? How very dare you. Can't you see how cute these guys are? Am I to believe that as they grow, all my happiness will dissolve as it sinks in just how 'impaired' they are?

I think some people really do sink into despair at this point. But at this juncture I was just a bit resentful instead. I thought, I'll find a better answer to my questions.

That's it. That's how I became an owl.

Finding better answers meant trawling through a lot of literature provided by the very helpful National Autistic Society. What did these children do that was different and why did they do it? Wow, it was all so complicated.

I went through reams of material, underlining the traits that I recognised and writing notes against those that I didn't. Lots of question marks, lots of asterisks, a few highlighter pens bit the dust...

I soon realised that autism isn't a diagonal graph but a series of peaks and troughs. Or, if you prefer a foodie analogy, it's more of a pick 'n' mix (which is what you get in cinemas when you buy different types of loose sweets). Although there's a collection of traits that are always present in everyone with autism, there's a further selection of behaviours and traits that affect some but not others.

What your kid does or doesn't do may be affected by many different factors, including their personality of course. But autism doesn't look the same in any two people. As the saying goes, 'When you've met one person with autism...you've met one person with autism.'

'Triad of Impairments' may be a useful term to the clinical observer, but parents aren't clinical. We are soft, warm human creatures who love our little offspring so much that we are very vulnerable. To be hit over the head with the news that your child is impaired in three major ways is very, very tough.

This would be bad enough, were it not for the fact that the Triad isn't the whole picture. For every impairment, there's also an attribute.

Not everyone with autism is a genius with an amazing memory, but not every 'impairment' turns out to be to someone's detriment either.

And the upside of autism? It seems no one mentions that at diagnosis stage. We focus on the bad news because we're being shown a path that deviates from the norm.

And maybe there is no choice but to do that when you're learning about something.

But I'm more than ten years into this now and I have a very different attitude. Having a diagnosis of autism for your child helps you to understand a raft of difficulties and it's very helpful for supporting people as they go through their education. But it shouldn't feel depressing.

What you're living with is a path less trodden – and yes, it is sometimes thorny, but it's not wrong.

So, I have my diagnosis but then my reams of information tell me that the situation is more pick 'n' mix.

Armed with this knowledge, I decided that the delightful, giggly twosome had not been magically changed by some bad witch, despite their label.

In the face of such an overwhelming amount of information, we decided to proceed one step at a time – focusing on our own difficulties and finding solutions to them.

After an exhausting amount of reading, I decided that there was far too much going on in the world of autism to learn absolutely everything.

No, what I'd do is focus on OUR autism. Our own pick 'n' mix selection. And to be honest, I wasn't bothered about everyone else's.

If anyone reading this is new to autism, I suggest you do the same.

The best bit about learning loads about autism over the years is that sooner or later you get confident enough to question some of the received wisdom. So, upset by what the term 'Triad of Impairments' was doing to our parent readers, co-editor Tori Houghton and I reworked the idea and constructed the Autism Sundae Dessert (using the same abbreviation as my much-hated term Autism Spectrum Disorder – see what we did there?) as an alternative way of explaining autism. This was our most popular feature by far and is now used in teaching and support groups.

What's in the Autism Sundae Dessert? You'll have to read on to find out.

I do love a cliff-hanger…

2 Autism Can Change

Looking beyond the traditional definition

Age eight, to celebrate his parents' anniversary, Bobby has announced that he's offering a FREE trial to ALL his babysitters.

Bobby and Alec both have autism. That, my friends, is where their similarities end.

Alec is an adrenalin junkie, Bobby a computer whizz. Bobby is quiet and thoughtful and sees food merely as fuel. Alec is loud and mischievous and if you bribe him with food he'll do just about anything. Signing 'biscuit' is not that easy in Makaton sign language – it involves tapping the left elbow with your right hand, so requires co-ordinating both sides of your body. Alec's fine motor skills were seriously impeded by his accident. Yet, strangely, this sign was never a problem. If signing 'biscuit' had involved climbing a ladder in flip flops, he'd have done it. The 'cake' sign is also not an issue.

Alec is thin and gangly and eats chocolate and cake. Some things in life just aren't fair.

Alec loves the outdoors, while sky and grass is a bit of a novelty for Bobby. My husband, Gavin, has a running joke when Bobby sidles out into the garden. 'Bobby! How great to see you! Look – what's that blue stuff? Sky! Fluffy things? Clouds!'

'Ha ha, Dad, very funny,' says Bobby (getting the joke – good stuff), settling down with his iPad. Fresh air is all very well as long as Wi-Fi is nearby.

This difference is in part down to the twins' varying natures but also down to their different physical experiences of the environment. So how do we explain the similarities in people with autism to the outside world, while accepting that everyone's different?

Plus, if you think explaining autism to other people is difficult, imagine explaining it to your own kid. Some parents are so worried that they'll sound negative that they don't tackle it at all. Besides, how are children supposed to understand that their friend who doesn't talk has the same condition as them, when they talk all the time? It's so confusing!

The downbeat nature of the Triad means that parents are obliged to rely on their own skill and judgement to make autism sound palatable and not damage a little person's self-esteem. That's even more difficult if you're not feeling that great about the diagnosis yourself.

The Autism Sundae Dessert

The Autism Sundae Dessert (copyright us at *AuKids* magazine, ahem) was invented to address these difficulties and define autism for the modern age.

Co-editor Tori and I demonstrate this Autism Sundae Dessert with coloured salt dough and flavoured sauces at conferences, because we always fancied the idea of being children's TV presenters but never got the chance.

We did try ice-cream, but it melted rather quickly and not all conference centres have freezers. Believe me, we have suffered a few liquefied disasters in developing this concept.

So, imagine you are sitting in front of us and we have our aprons on. Tori, wearing a Madonna-style microphone headset, has already warmed up before you arrived with a quick rendition of the movements to the song 'Vogue'. Meanwhile, I can't be trusted with handling any materials and talking at the same time, because I'm clumsy. I am therefore in charge of the commentary.

To make an Autism Sundae Dessert, you first need a sundae glass. This represents personality.

Why does autism vary so much? Because people vary so much. Shy and retiring? (Wobble one glass in front of people.) You may avoid people altogether – sensing that you lack social skills makes you even less willing to try. Outgoing? (Wobble other glass in front of people.) You might not care as much and strike up a conversation with just anyone, making you equally vulnerable, especially when it comes to the internet. Both personalities have difficulties with social skills, but their behaviour is different.

Once you have your glass, you add three scoops of ice-cream. A Neapolitan ice-cream represents the universally recognisable triad of autism – difficulty with communication (chocolate), social interaction (vanilla) and flexibility of thought (strawberry).

The size of those ice-cream scoops varies from person to person. Bobby has a larger scoop of strawberry than Alec because Bobby is more rigid in his behaviour and routines. Alec has a larger scoop of chocolate than Bobby because his communication needs are greater. Although these three elements are the same in everyone who has autism, their proportions will vary widely.

The size of the ice-cream scoops can also change according to different environments. For instance, in a crowded and noisy environment, Bobby's vanilla scoop of ice-cream (social skills) will suddenly get larger – it will become more of an issue for him. When relaxed at home, the autism will seem very different, hardly detectable at all sometimes.

Time plays a role, too. With maturity and intervention, those scoops may change size.

This is something that tends to confuse many people about autism. At diagnosis, you are told your child has a life-long condition and it seems you're stuck with it. No one told me that although autism doesn't disappear, it does change over time, quite radically. I wish they had.

With a bit of intervention, social skills improve. With great strategies, thinking can start to become less rigid. Even without any of these, experience and maturity all work their magic over time.

If you're a parent reading this, I'm telling you now, in an arrogant as heck way, autism is no rigid brick. Autism is mouldable, like clay, and you have the power to mould it so that your child's difficulties will affect them less, leaving those positive aspects of autism to shine freely.

Autism is mouldable, like clay, and you have the power to mould it so that your child's difficulties will affect them less, leaving those positive aspects of autism to shine freely.

And, just like clay, if you do leave it too long, then certain behaviour can become hardened and set. Moulding it in the early years helps tremendously. But don't feel you must do it all in the next few days. The things that I am going to tell you about need no special skills, it's just tweaking your parenting style – that's it.

So, we have our changeable scoops of ice-cream and now it's time for the fun bit. Chocolate sauce. We use chocolate sauce to represent sensory difficulties. Sensory difficulties have until recently been a bit of an afterthought when it came to describing autism. That's because they don't fit conveniently into the Triad. Sensory difficulties are in fact central to autism – they underpin many of the difficulties that the ice-cream scoops represent.

Sensory difficulties are in fact central to autism – they underpin many of the difficulties that the ice-cream scoops represent.

Sensory difficulties mean that the way a person processes their environment through any of the senses is in some way different from the norm. You can't be a great communicator or be very flexible, for instance, if it feels as if your environment is attacking you.

Wait a sec, I'm going to turn down the heating in this room until you are freezing cold. Then I'll turn up some music until it's so loud you can't concentrate. Feeling sociable? Feeling communicative? Feeling flexible? Thought not.

We use chocolate sauce in our ice-cream sundae because sensory issues cover the other elements of autism to the extent that you may not be able to tell much about the underlying traits. It's only when you deal with a person's environment, find out what's bothering them and adapt it to suit them that you can see a person's true potential.

> It's only when you deal with a person's environment, find out what's bothering them and adapt it to suit them that you can see a person's true potential.

Strawberry sauce is next and it represents that wonderful term 'co-morbid conditions'. In other words, other conditions that your child may have alongside autism. We need to acknowledge them, since they make the picture a little less clear.

The more you know about autism, the more you realise that its boundaries really aren't as solid as people like to think. Its definition is just convenient, but there is no medical test for autism. It quite often overlaps with other conditions, such as ADHD

(Attention Deficit Hyperactivity Disorder) and OCD (Obsessive-Compulsive Disorder). We add strawberry sauce to acknowledge that if you have another condition, it makes your autism traits harder to separate out.

The Autism Sundae Dessert carries an optional wafer or Cadbury's Flake. If you're not from the UK, a wafer is a thin biscuit that we push inside an ice-cream and a Cadbury's Flake is a stick of chocolate that can be added, too. We usually buy a packet of these for a conference, because we know that if we don't, we won't have any left by the time we get to the demo.

The Flake represents behavioural issues. Some people think that behavioural issues are part of autism. The Flake is here to indicate that it's NOT part of the sundae. It can be added or taken away.

This is because behavioural difficulties are a secondary issue with autism, not a primary one. If your experience of the environment is overloading and if your social experience with other people is anxiety-provoking, you are likely, sooner or later, to get extremely upset. This isn't caused by the autism itself, but by an environment that doesn't cater for it. Autistic people aren't intrinsically aggressive, but aggression can be a natural reaction to finding yourself under threat.

If we appreciate social and sensory difficulties, plus frustrations caused by lack of language, and we adjust accordingly, then behavioural 'issues' are by no means inevitable. When autistic people become aggressive because of their environment, some people call it 'challenging behaviour'. There are entire courses dedicated to helping us parents get to the root of it, since it causes so much confusion and upset. Yet calling your child 'challenging' can predispose you to a negative frame of mind about why they act out when they do. Truly, no one actually wants to have a meltdown. Autism expert Phoebe Caldwell (2014a) hit the nail on the head when she said, 'It's not challenging behaviour, it's distressed behaviour.' Understand autism and you can do away with the Flake a lot of the time. But not all the time: we all lose our temper sometimes, autistic or not.

And what about the essential parts of autism that are brilliant? Fantastic recall. Enduring passions. Honesty. Attention to detail. Original thinking. Visual thinking. Being great with computers for some or maths for others. Dedication. Loyalty. Lack of pretence. Lack of subterfuge. Whatever it is, these positive aspects are represented by sprinkles on the sundae.

A cherry on the top is optional and represents an autism savant. That is, someone who has exceptional abilities in a certain area. Daniel Tammet is an example of a mathematical savant. Stephen Wiltshire, who draws entire cityscapes from memory, is another example of a truly gifted individual. We don't all have this decoration, but just in case, it's an optional extra.

Besides, a lot of autistic people spend an overwhelming amount of time and energy on a single passion – this makes them into an expert, even if they aren't a 'savant'. Cherry for them.

Our Autism Sundae Dessert is now complete.

At this point I am usually covered in chocolate sauce and so is the microphone. Tori waits a nanosecond after the applause is over and then scoffs the demonstration Flake.

What we hadn't realised when coming up with the sundae is how useful it would be for explaining autism to children.

'What type of ice-cream sundae am I?' asked Bobby as he looked at our Autism Sundae Dessert poster one morning.

'Well, you've got a small scoop of chocolate, a slightly larger scoop of vanilla and a slightly larger scoop of strawberry.'

'Do I have any chocolate sauce?'

'Yep, you have some don't you because you have sensitive hearing.'

'I have sprinkles, right?'

'You have LOADS of sprinkles!'

In the last school holidays, Bobby painted his own Autism Sundae Dessert. Not usually a keen artist, and somewhat hindered by a bristle brush large enough to paint a fence, he nevertheless reproduced a surrealist bird's-eye view of the Autism Sundae Dessert. Then he drew Pokémon figures around it. This, he was proud to say, represented him.

In this way, kids get to realise that autism isn't like a bump on the knee. It's a part of your personality, growing and changing with you.

Judy Garland once said, 'Always be a first-rate version of yourself, instead of a second-rate version of somebody else' (Aronson 1997).

It's important for kids to recognise that their autism plays a part in who they are and doesn't remove anything from them.

However well-meaning our definition, most people really don't get what you're talking about until you put it in a meaningful context.

That's what this book is about, explaining what this entire Autism Sundae Dessert looks like in the real world.

You can't just talk about autism in abstract terms and expect people to get it. It's important that you mention actual human beings at some point. I've been to a few conferences where you'd never know that autism affected real people.

When I used to explain autism at Bobby's school, I did so by mentioning an aspect of autism followed by an example of how that translated in Bobby's behaviour and what to do about it.

Since autism isn't just a thing but also a part of a person and their personality, you must relate it to your own child in this way, otherwise huge assumptions can be made.

'Don't worry, I've had a boy with autism in my class before. I know all about it.'

'Well one of my mates has bright red hair so why can't she write songs like Ed Sheeran?' I never say because I haven't got the guts or the wit at the time.

That sundae does not look the same in everyone.

But before you reach for your ice-cream scoop, just freeze a minute (see what I did there?). I am describing the terminology that was used when my twins were diagnosed, but there has been a recent update to replace the idea of the Triad.

There will be those of you reading this thinking, 'But what about the new DSM-5 criteria?'

DSM is short for *Diagnostic and Statistical Manual of Mental Disorders*, in which autism is listed and defined. In the latest version, the DSM-5 (American Psychiatric Association 2013), quite a few changes were made to the definition of autism. Instead of the idea of a Triad, the new definition describes a collection of symptoms including social communication, behaviour, flexibility and sensory sensitivity. Sensory issues, thankfully, are now far more recognised.

Since 2013, different conditions related to autism (like Asperger's), fall under the single term 'Autism Spectrum Disorder'.

This has upset many with Asperger Syndrome, who have forged their own identity. They still call themselves Aspies. I could go on for ages about how Asperger's differs from autism, but it's not really my place to.

To avoid the difficulties caused by the term Autism Spectrum Disorder referring to people with such a varying range of abilities, there are now three levels. Level 1 requires the least amount of support, Level 2 a little more and Level 3 is a person requiring the highest amount of support in order to function.[1]

I'll be honest, I don't like the terminology surrounding autism. I didn't like the old terminology and I'm not a heck of a lot keener on the new. It gives parents no sense of the movement of autism or the development of an individual.

In quite a crude sense, the new levels work when referring to functioning. The problem is that, once again,

---

1   This website explains the new levels of autism according to the DSM-5 very well: www.verywell.com/what-are-the-three-levels-of-autism-260233.

they present autism as a solid brick, something incapable of changing.

Also, when you don't know the DSM-5 definition inside out, a lot can be lost in translation. Simplification when it comes to autism may be useful for clinicians, but it can cause laypeople to make assumptions. The generalisation of autism into 'low' and 'high' levels can cause people to make mistakes when it comes to the detail.

When I spoke about autism as a pick 'n' mix in Chapter 1, I described it that way because, in my view, autism doesn't come as a hierarchy.

Maybe you want people to know that your son has 'high-functioning autism' because you need them to know that he is bright and hasn't got learning difficulties.

Or you might want to tell people that your daughter's autism is 'severe' because you need people to know how disabling her condition is for her.

Let's assume that a 'high-functioning' person with autism can talk and goes to a mainstream school, like my son Bobby. He has no learning difficulties. Yet in certain environments, his functioning can substantially drop because of stress and pressure. Level 1 allows for that, but if in daily conversation you mark Bobby with the glib expression 'high functioning' (because most people aren't familiar with Level 1) you may just assume that socially he is a bit quirky. You will have no idea of how hard he works, and how much insight it takes him, to keep himself functioning at that level in a mainstream environment.

Also, according to the new DSM-5 criteria, Bobby has shifted levels in the last ten years through maturity, insight, learning and intervention. I don't know how this situation would be handled were he facing diagnosis today.

On the other hand, what do we understand by 'severe autism'? Lots of sensory issues causing shutdowns or meltdowns? Lack of language? Special school?

Well, what about the likes of Naoki Higashida, who wrote the now famous book *The Reason I Jump*, translated from Japanese to English by David Mitchell (Higashida and Mitchell 2014)? Naoki presents as being really 'severe' – in fact, he doesn't look as if he can keep still for a second.

Yet with stunning perseverance and the aid of technology, he managed to articulate with depth and insight all the difficulties that people like him experience. So, you can be extremely bright but require the highest level of support. If we label those sorts of people in a certain way, we must be careful that others don't underestimate them.

Jargon used by some professionals (sometimes unwittingly) may provide a common language and useful distinctions for clinicians. In ordinary life, it distances people from the subject of the conversation. Worse, it elevates some and in doing so it demotes others. Worse even than that, it can be inaccurate shorthand.

Don't let jargon be used as a smokescreen to bamboozle you. My rule of thumb is that if two people can speak the same jargon together, that's fine. If one of you is speaking it and the other cannot, that's not fine. That's creating an unhelpful imbalance in the relationship.

This applies whether you're a clued-up parent trying to get one over on an unhelpful teacher or you're a highly trained clinician speaking to an unversed parent.

When you tell people about your child's autism, describe exactly how it affects them and why. Ditch the jargon. Ditch words like 'high functioning' or 'severe' or 'classic'. If someone uses them on you, ask them what they really mean by that term. If they genuinely know what they're talking about, they will be able to tell you in simpler terms.

> My rule of thumb is that if two people can speak the same jargon together, that's fine. If one of you is speaking it and the other cannot, that's not fine. That's creating an unhelpful imbalance in the relationship.

Well, basic explanations it turns out can be just as confusing as complex ones. It's much better to scoop beyond the surface of the sundae and look at what's really going on.

Head to the freezer for some ice-cream and I'll see you in Chapter 3.

3 You Can't Compare Apples with Oranges (or You Can, but it's Fruitless)

Accepting them for who they are

Age eight, at the play centre, Bobby made his introductions: 'This is my mum, Debby, she's the co-founder of AuKids magazine. This is Alec, my brother, he's a giant.'

Before we talk about various aspects of autism and how they translate Chez Elley, I'd like to wander off the path slightly in order to properly introduce you to our twins, Bobby and Alec.

Meet Bobby

Bobby, as he politely informed me one morning, is Robert for short. I'm glad he told me that; it's not like I was there at his birth or anything.

The idea was that we'd call him 'Rob' for short. We ended up shortening it in all sorts of ways – Bob, Rob, Bobby, Bobster, Robster-dobster…until our first speech and language therapist pointed out that this might be confusing and we should settle on calling him just one name. 'Bobby' was the name he seemed to prefer, so that's the one he uses.

Bobby nearly had his very own book. He still might. The 'Bobbyisms' that head some of my chapters are just snippets of his daily wisdom. Since he didn't learn language in the usual way, he makes up his own words and phrases and some of them (like 'dia-horror' for diarrhoea, 'dreadline' for deadline and 'Tabasco bath' referring to too much hot water) should genuinely be considered for the *Oxford English Dictionary*. His honesty, combined with very literal thinking and a tendency to do things his way and no one else's, make him very refreshing company.

Bobby has his own ideas about success and his ambition is to become a YouTube millionaire. That's my ambition for him, too, to be honest. He's a superb gamer and not a bad presenter. I've no idea how much room there is for these sorts of experts but I figure one with autism might just have a niche in the market.

As well as being a great programmer and gamer, Bobby can remember 721 Pokémon and their evolved forms, which must come in handy at some point.

He is hilarious and has a sweet and caring nature. Alec often takes a swipe at him and he ducks with supreme agility, rarely fighting back. As he's become aware of his brother's differences, he has steadily become more reliable at rounding him up and spotting signs of trouble around the house for me.

This responsible side has only developed within the last few years but boy am I glad of it. Although, if I do ask him to do anything and he's winning at Mario, I get asked, 'Am I your slave, now?', which is a genuine query.

There is another person we should mention and that's Pikachu. Bobby's toy Pikachu accompanies him everywhere. When he's swimming, Pikachu watches from the side. When he's doing exams, Pikachu sits on his lap. Bobby's even run cross-country with Pikachu under his arm.

A cousin gave Pikachu to Bobby when he was about nine and since then they've only been parted briefly for Pikachu's monthly outings to the washing machine.

We have tried convincing Bobby that pocket Pikachu may be easier. We have tried getting a mini evolved form of Pikachu, a Raichu, to take over. Out of earshot, Gavin has occasionally suggested that we 'lose' Pikachu by drop-kicking him over the fence. Still, Bobby won't give Pikachu up.

Pikachu is a bit like Bobby's avatar. I think in some deep way he has become connected to Bobby's soul. And let's be fair, I have bigger fish to fry than parting him from his comfort toy.

Sometimes, I think Bobby knows what he's doing taking Pikachu everywhere with him. Of course, you can't spot autism from a distance and Pikachu has become Bobby's way of saying, 'Cut me some slack, I feel younger than my age.'

The entire school knows that Bobby is the kid with Pikachu and so it's got legendary status now. It even appeared on the class photo, and among the peers' names beneath, written in supremely posh italics, were 'Bobby Elley and Pikachu', which I thought showed just what a fantastic school it is. By the way, if you're thinking about the other parents, they were given the non-Pikachu option, too.

When it comes to keeping up with trends, Bobby isn't materialistic in the least. You'll find lack of materialism quite common in autistic people, because they're not concerned about how they look to others. Show me an autistic poser and I'll show you someone who isn't autistic.

This lack of materialism wasn't really evident until Bobby became a teenager. Now, when everyone else is concerned with fitting in (and wants whatever their peers have got), Bobby couldn't care less. If life is a competition, no one told him. If he wants to go to school with his trousers left inside his socks, he will do. Sniff.

You know all that stuff we try to teach children about valuing individuality and originality, about not being a sheep and following the crowd? Autistic people have mastered that naturally. While most of us fall into line sooner or later, this is one of the reasons why so many scientific breakthroughs were discovered by autistic people. They aren't influenced as easily by others and when they love something, they stick at it.

If we shore up their self-belief, value their differences and stop trying to make them be like everyone for 40 seconds, we'll see that we have some very original thinkers on our hands.

So there.

Bobby is refreshing in how little he cares about his image. Whenever I try to persuade him into a trendy top, Bobby says, 'You don't have to look cool to be cool, Mum,' and, once again, I realise I am in the presence of a small Buddha.

That said, having been unconcerned about what's in his piggy bank in terms of getting the latest trend, the minute a new Mario game is launched (actually about a year before its launch thanks to the internet), Bobby suddenly wants a tenner for getting out of bed in the morning. There's also a new willingness to do jobs around the house (for a fee), combined with a daily interest in how many months it is until his birthday and Christmas. Unfortunately for Bobby, his birthday and Christmas fall in the same month.

Bobby's stoic nature impresses me. He doesn't whine for attention. In fact, because of the emotional overload that his autism gives him, heaps of attention is something he doesn't like much; he recently had a really bad day when they all tried cheering him in Physical Education. If he has a rubbish day at school, he dusts himself off and starts again undeterred. This is quite unusual for autistic kids who often hold it together until they get home.

On the rare occasions when another child has said something hurtful, Bobby refuses to label them a bully, instead pointing out that they just need to be educated in autism.

Again, this lack of judging others is one of many positive autistic traits, caused by difficulty in generalising. If others were to label one 'bad attitude moment' as bullying, Bobby would just see it as one bad moment.

When a particularly obnoxious little boy in primary school called Bobby a 'flappy bird' thanks to his hand flapping, it was designed to be a taunt. Bobby didn't merely rain on his parade, he cancelled it due to flooding, by replying, 'Yes! I'm a flappy bird! Ha ha!' and flapping. There's nothing so disempowering for a bully as someone who can laugh at themselves.

Anyhow, there's really no point in bullying Bobby because he believes the best about people, so he'd not suspect anyone of being deliberately nasty, as it isn't in his own nature.

Being aware that what's in another person's head isn't the same as what's in your own is called Theory of Mind and it's something that autistic people tend to lack. In this way, Bobby's autism makes him vulnerable but is also a sound defence from getting hurt.

I'll come to Theory of Mind later in this book. As with many aspects of autism, lacking something naturally doesn't mean you can't develop it, you just have to be made aware of it more consciously. What you don't know instinctively, you can make up for in learning.

Anxiety (caused by a core aspect of autism, rigidity of thought, making you less adaptable) is Bobby's main issue, but he is persistently cheerful in the face of it, even if it does sometimes get him down.

Bobby loves his autism. The other day, he tried to pack a load of fairy books into his schoolbag. He arrived late to fantasy fiction, not really getting it until he was about nine, but is now mesmerised by little worlds and develops his own imaginary landscapes constantly. If you thought lack of imagination was part of autism, it's a myth.

'Bobby, aren't you worried people will think that's a bit girlie?' I said. 'No. They know that I'm awesome and unique,' he pointed out matter of factly, as he stuffed a dozen twinkly fairy covers into his schoolbag.

Positive about autism? Job done, I thought, mentally dusting off my hands and wondering whether this meant I could now take some time off. A couple of years or so.

Bobby's positive view of autism is down to the fact that he's always known he was on the spectrum and that it was presented to him as not only the cause of certain difficulties, but also the reason why he is so 'unique' and can do things that others can't.

That wasn't a fib to protect his feelings; that was the truth.

Our first inkling of the upside of his condition (we hadn't been told there may be benefits) came when it became apparent that Bobby could read before he could speak. It's called hyperlexia and many kids on the spectrum have it. He didn't learn to read in the usual way, building up letter sounds. He just 'saw' the words as a pattern. His primary teacher was initially concerned that this would affect his reading and his ability to understand what he read, but this didn't prove to be the case.

Bobby's great memory became useful as he got a bit older, when he would request a Mr Men book and then tell us the number it was in the series (1–47). This saved heaps of time looking through the bookshelf and earned him the title 'The Ninja' among his cousins.

I explained Bobby's autism initially when he was about six by telling him that his brain worked brilliantly in some ways and struggled a little in others. I didn't weigh him down with too much detail – no point. If it looks like a concern to you, it'll feel like a concern to them. This is not just one conversation after all; it's many, which have developed over the years.

Autistic people find it hard to understand abstract concepts, so I've always found it easier to illustrate autism just after Bobby's thoughts and behaviour have perplexed him. If he worried about a change of routine, I'd explain that this was caused by his autism and that we just needed to put things in place to help him get around those problems. In talking about those difficulties caused by autism (rather than him), we maintained his self-belief.

When Bobby was two years old, he wouldn't ack-nowledge you if you walked into a room. Friends felt like ghosts as they tried tactfully to get his attention. He didn't respond to his name or questions.

He spoke late, at the age of nearly four, and used repetitive speech for many years. Conversation didn't develop naturally but through a gradual process of teaching him the essential elements of one.

I often say that, when you have a child with autism, it's like being given a Lego® construction kit. Whereas other children may have pre-fabricated conversation skills, you need to start building pretty much from scratch. How you do that isn't complicated, it's just a series of clear explanations as you go along. How we do things, and why.

I often say that, when you have a child with autism, it's like being given a Lego® construction kit.

It was the same for social skills. Life when Bobby was small was a bit like a cookery programme. While others just cook, I'd be giving a running commentary on ingredients needed and how you combine them.

Praise for getting things right – in conversation and in social skills – worked wonders, as it gave Bobby a solid basis from which to work. It always saddens me when I hear parents telling off children, autistic or not. There is nothing in 'don't' that tells you what you should be doing instead.

The best part of my day is the evenings, when Bobby is ready for bed and we have a chat. Here he is relaxed and there are no extra pressures. I am in constant awe of someone who couldn't initially string a single sentence together when he started school but can now chat happily about his life and ask me questions about how I feel. Teachers say that Bobby is one of the most self-aware autistic students they have. It blows my mind. It makes me feel happy in a way I can't describe.

It's all such a far cry from the future I had originally imagined after the Triad news. Whatever happens next, Bobby is already a success to me.

Meet Alec

I wasn't thinking about his biography when we named Alec. In a shallow move that I'm not particularly proud of, we called him after Sean Bean's character Alec Trevelyan in the James Bond film *GoldenEye*.

Alec finds his own name really difficult to say and I'm sort of cursing myself for not calling him Bobby. He attempts it boldly in exchange for a Dad tickle (not a Mum tickle, btw, which is very much Second-Class Entertainment). When he makes an 'A' sound he looks like a baby tiger. He struggles with the 'L' sound, though, which requires more complex motor planning. When you have a non-speaking child, the complexity of shaping individual letters amazes you.

Alec's accident has moulded our entire lives and it's defined the way we bring him up, too.

In September 2006, as the one-year anniversary of his accident approached, I felt a sense of dread. The weather started to change, became semi-autumnal, a mix of summer sun and crisp air. Even thinking of it now brings about a shudder. You can forget what day it is, but your body instinctively tunes into the season. It was a horrible day and I was glad when it was over.

On the second anniversary of the accident, I decided we had to do something about it. But what to do? We could try to forget it, but it would be there all the same, sitting in the corner of the day waiting for a pause in the action.

I came up with an idea. Instead of dreading the date, we could dress it up as a party and treat it a bit like a second birthday. Paddington has one and so does the Queen (unfortunate order I put that in), so why not Alec? We called the day Survival Day and every year since, we've taken the boys for a slap-up meal. On Survival Day, Alec can eat as much ice-cream as he wants. Ben and Jerry's have declared it a national holiday. Okay, not really.

Alec's Survival Day celebrates the fact that he is alive and happy as heck, rather than focusing on what might have been had he not had an accident.

We apply this thinking to all aspects of Alec's life. Every achievement is a brilliant surprise and we don't focus on what he can't do. Not being super-human, I can't do that 100 per cent of the time, but if I can do it 90 per cent of the time, I find it helps.

I don't compare Alec with his peers, or even with Bobby, and nor does Gavin. We think purely about his own life. The only thing that matters to us is that Alec continues to do things that he couldn't do before.

This is, in my view, the key to anybody's happiness, not just ours. Facebook encourages us to live our lives like a price-comparison website. It makes you miserable. My Grandma Sophie had a gift for loving what she already had in life (which wasn't much), focusing on love and music, and I always admired it. It took Alec's accident to teach me the same.

When Alec first went to Valley School, our local special school, at the age of five, I asked what PMLD stood for. The teacher said 'Profound and Multiple Learning Disabilities' and I felt like I'd been hit with a stun gun. We were so used to looking at Alec's own progress and not comparing him with anyone else that this label had never occurred to us.

'Is it really that bad?' I thought, tearfully. But then you only have to look at Alec, grinning away, and you realise that it isn't that bad at all. Because, frankly, Alec couldn't give a monkey's what PMLD means. Alec would no doubt believe that it meant Person Who Most Loves Doughnuts. Alec is just Alec. He does realise that he's different, of course, but I don't think he spends long moments in his bedroom pondering the nature of the universe.

If you catch yourself doing this type of 'why are they different?' pondering as a parent, I think you've got to ask yourself whether being different is actually a problem for the little person in question. Alec's having the best life – he really has a great time, unencumbered by worries and predictions about the future. He lives in the moment.

In fact, Alec has taught me two things: the art of mindfulness and the art of patience. They go hand in hand. If Alec had a motto, it would be, 'What's the rush?' This motto is particularly aggravating at 8.20am on a Monday morning, when he's ambling towards the car, rotating a piece of string around his finger, with all the urgency of someone about to go on a country drive through the Lake District.

As I push his behind into the front seat sufficiently to slam the door behind it, I tell myself that he's got it right and I have got it wrong. There is no rush. Time is an abstract notion. Grit teeth. My philosophy is shattered by Bobby, who stands at the front door shouting, 'Mum, where are my shoes?'

We were sitting in Alec's bedroom last summer when I noticed him gaze into the air. Following his eye line, I realised that he was looking at dust particles floating through sunbeams. I stopped what I was doing and watched them, too. It was a bit like a gentle, slow, indoor snow (mental note that the vacuuming needs doing). I could see why he found it captivating. His lack of urgency may be frustrating in some ways but is a real lesson in others.

We filter out so many ordinary miracles, driven by what we view as worthy achievement. Later in life, people spend large sums going to retreats to undo this type of thinking in order to get in touch with the real world.

But Alec is already there with mindfulness; he's the most in-touch person I know. His inability to filter out what we would term irrelevance in his surroundings may hold him back, but it also makes him appreciate life very deeply.

Alec has grit and determination, oodles of it. It's what got him into trouble in the first place, but it's helped him master motor skills that he had to relearn after his accident.

He also has an inner intelligence that people often miss because they only see a disabled child with a slightly uneven gait and a lopsided grin. That inner intelligence is starting to show as he communicates more, and the signs of it are everywhere, from the way he turns a pear around in the fruit bowl so that you don't know he's taken a bite, to his self-assumed role of navigator in the car, working the indicator correctly for the entire journey and reminding you when you should be in third gear.

I'm so glad I never underestimated him.

Non-verbal, sensory seeker, heart-winner, that's Alec. Long eyelashes, large eyes, a mischievous dimple and a generally easy-going attitude that has won over many fans who might otherwise be impatient because of his Lake-District attitude to timing.

Alec finds a lot of things funny when I can't see the joke. As with many autistic people, if he finds something funny once, it doesn't cease to be funny even after 200 times.

On one occasion, it was the word 'spoon' in his spelling game that tickled him. He kept pressing for the word, then doing his inside-out laugh. I don't know why. I just wish it took this little to make me laugh out loud.

Oh, and by the way, Alec is also the only person I know who can make himself laugh by tickling himself. I didn't think that was physically possible.

Alec won't ever live independently and he'll never be given an executive title (unless it's Chief Biscuit Tester). We don't mind. By being here at all, he has already made us proud and achieved more than I could have done, given what he's been through.

One of my talks is called the Ten Commandments of Raising an Autistic Child. My favourite commandment is Thou Shalt Not Compare.

Of all the things that I've seen make parents most miserable, it's comparing their child with others. It happens all the time – at school, at playgroups, in conversation – people talk about where their children are up to; it's natural.

It's not necessary to join in, though, or feel somehow lacking if your child isn't developmentally at the same level. You are on a whole different playing field or, to use another metaphor, other children are apples, ours are oranges. *Your child is not sub-standard; they are different.* As a good friend of mine said recently, they're not broken, they were built that way.

If you're expecting an apple, you'll be disappointed.

Accept you've got an orange instead and life becomes so much simpler.

4 Happiness Comes from Perspective

Living with a label

*Age eight, you know that Bobby's been in trouble
when he asks, 'Is skating on thin ice actually safe?'*

The saying goes, 'If life gives you lemons, make lemonade.'

Life had chucked me a couple of oranges and I don't mind orangeade one bit. Would I accept the twins as they were or mourn the apples that never fell our way?

It was quite a straightforward decision, really. Alec's accident had given us enough battles to last a lifetime. I didn't want to struggle; I wanted to accept. But to accept, I first needed to face some fears – head on.

When you only let reality in through a narrow gap in the wall, it becomes a blinding shaft of light that's painful to face. The irony is that when you smash the wall down and meet it head on, it diffuses and isn't nearly as scary as you might think.

I had my first dose of genuine reality in 1999, when I decided that I was going to develop my little hobby of writing in-house newsletters for every workplace I joined and become a full-time journalist.

New Year's resolutions can mean empty promises, but a turn-of-the-century one, it turned out, proved to be defining. A week before the year 2000, I bought the book *Life Strategies* by Dr Phil McGraw (1999), a regular on *The Oprah Winfrey Show*. I was hoping it would give me the direction I needed and, boy, did it.

After a couple of un-lucrative freelance jobs and a lousy volunteer stint (a week's work experience for a national women's magazine being a low point), I took a job editing the village news at a weekly title, the *Wiltshire Gazette and Herald*. From there, I worked my way up to the role of sub-editor. I was let loose on the arts section and within two years of reading Phil's book, was happily ensconced in my dream job, editing news and writing film reviews.

I honestly couldn't believe it, but the whole thing had resulted from one simple lesson: getting real.

Phil is the king of saying it like it is, and within the first chapter, his words were already slapping me round the head with a good dose of realism.

He revealed all the tricks that people play to avoid facing the truth: looking at what they think they see or what they hope to see, but never actually what they are really seeing. This stops them from realising their goals in life, because their world view is largely inaccurate.

I stood tall, braced myself and prepared to unveil the truth. Examining my fears and questioning my assumptions about my dream job was one of the most empowering things I have ever done.

I realised that I'd played a lot of negative tapes in my head, telling myself that I'd never be a writer, that these things happened to other people, that I hadn't gone through the proper channels and that at 30, it was way too late to change any of this.

Phil stopped me dead in my tracks. His book demanded I sat up and listened. It turned out I was wandering around in a lonely castle constructed from my own homespun falsehoods.

I dared to question myself. What fear was each of those thoughts based on? Did I have enough knowledge to make those assumptions? Was I actually just guessing, because I didn't have the answers and finding out might be too difficult?

How did I know, for instance, that every journalist on the planet had completed a degree in journalism? Had I asked them? It was just my assumption. My own degree, in English Language and Literature, was hardly irrelevant.

I hadn't even been aware of these little fictions, but once I noticed their presence, I knocked down the entire castle, realising that my reality, although comforting, was based on no foundation whatsoever.

I then constructed a new reality, based on actual knowledge, and I started to take real steps towards the future I'd dreamed about.

Why do we do this to ourselves, creating these fictional little tales? It lets us off the hook. With this tower of myths surrounding me, I'd never have to be brave enough to try to break out. I'd protect myself from my own failures.

The book taught me to identify where it was I needed to get to and to take gradual steps towards it, instead of leaving my head in the clouds.

Work experience aged 30 may have been a little humiliating, but it was a necessary step to build up evidence of my abilities.

And, by the way, to the self-obsessed prima donnas who bossed me around at the women's magazine that week and smirked at my dress sense, I'd just like to say, 'Ner ner ner ner ner.'

Fast forward to after our twins' diagnosis and I'd become used to regular reality checks whenever I felt I could be hiding something from myself. Each time I felt an uneasy sense of not wanting to think about something, I sat down and questioned my underlying fears and what shaky assumptions they were based on.

When it came to autism, I had to ask myself what I was most afraid of. I wasn't afraid of our twins being different, but I was afraid of them being unhappy. I was afraid of living a different kind of life that I knew nothing about. I was afraid that I wasn't up to the job. I was afraid of not knowing, of failing my children because I didn't have the information I needed in order to help them.

Most of all, I was afraid of not fitting into my own life anymore.

There, I'd faced it all. It boiled down to mostly one thing – lack of knowledge.

You already know, of course, that I became an owl. And as each fear was faced, gradually they disappeared.

There are answers – plenty of them – you just have to find them. Spend your energy on searching for reasons your kid does the things that they do – rather than wishing you had an apple instead of an orange – and it pays off.

When you start to understand their own reality, it all makes sense. Well, sort of. Most of the time. I'll tell you what I've learnt through doing this a bit later.

I had moved from negative to neutral – now it was time to ramp up a gear to positive.

Being an optimist, positive thinking is something that I've always had.

Translated into daily life with my twins, positive thinking means that I choose a perspective that keeps me in high spirits most of the time.

It helps me to recover from problems very quickly (it happened – get over it) and focus on solutions instead. It's also generated an energy that encourages everyone who works with Bobby and Alec to catch my enthusiasm. 'Hey, I've got a new idea – have we thought about trying this?' is much more energising than, 'Oh, we have that problem again. It's awful isn't it. How awful it is.'

If you introduce your kid with a sigh, it doesn't exactly breathe life into the day ahead. Pop through the door like a ray of sunshine on the other hand, and teachers kind of catch the vibe that your child's fun to be around and they run with it.

So, how do you do it, this positive thinking? Does it mean denying the reality of what you're faced with?

It doesn't, believe me. It all boils down to perspective.

I'm going to tell you a very boring story about my life. Later, it will become clear why I've shared this with you. So, don't worry, there is a point.

After a hard day looking after the twins, there's nothing I like more than to settle down to some rubbish TV. Between the hours of 4pm and 6pm in British households, quiz shows have become the undemanding introduction to a mid-week evening.

I'm not exactly loyal when it comes to quiz shows and I switch between competing channels. Over on Channel 4, I used to watch *Deal or No Deal*. In this quiz show, you can win £10,000. Yet even with such a huge prize, you could still end up in tears.

At its heart, *Deal or No Deal* is a gambling game, and if you check out too early and settle for a low sum of money, there is a chance that you could have won anything up to £250,000. That's why you could end up crying with a mere £10,000 to take home.

Over on the other side is its BBC rival show, *Pointless*, in which winning just £2,000 is an occasion for huge jubilation. Or it would be, but this is the BBC and instead you just shake the quiz master's hand heartily. On this well-mannered show, £2,000 is a very respectable jackpot indeed.

What's all this got to do with autism?

Well, it proves beyond all doubt that it's not what you have in life that has the power to make you happy but the perspective that you take on what you have.

In other words, it's not autism that controls you, but your perspective on it.

As First Lady of the United States, Martha Washington, so eloquently put it, 'The greater part of our happiness or misery depends on our dispositions and not on our circumstances. We carry the seeds of one or the other about with us in our minds wherever we go.'

Happiness isn't a constant state; it happens when something exceeds your expectations. Since you can determine what your own expectations are, it follows that you have the power to create your own happiness.

Now, I know it looks as if I've been reading too many self-help books, but this really does work.

I learnt the perspective lesson the tough way. When Alec nearly lost his life, my expectations were exceeded by his survival. We were told that the first 72 hours after his fall were critical. In those three days, the pendulum was going to swing one way or the other on his little life. Over that, we had no control.

After he made it through, we made a small deal with the universe that we had him back and wouldn't ask for too much more.

We never forgot that.

Our expectations had already been exceeded – but it was after this that I noticed other people talking about their children purely in terms of expectations.

It became clear to me that their happiness in their children was nearly always dictated by outside influences.

While mainstream parents were busy swishing exceeded academic expectations about, some of the autism parents I met were doing quite the opposite, fretting over developmental milestones that had yet to appear and ever prey to the fear that their kids were somehow sub-standard.

Well, the idea of sub-standard comes from comparing your 'orange' with everyone else's 'apple'. So, I wasn't going to play that game.

Alec had already exceeded our expectations and Bobby had too, since the Triad indicated that he was impaired and yet, apart from a lack of language, I couldn't see the problem. I still thought he was pretty much delightful and even a Ninja at times. No one was going to tell me otherwise.

Once we accepted that our twins were going their own way in life, not to be compared with anyone else's children, we started to make sensible decisions based on what was right for them, rather than what looked good to everyone else.

When it came to starting school, I didn't like to think of separating Bobby and Alec. But getting real had shown me that their needs were very different.

If Alec needed special school, then that was where he'd go. I knew for sure that Alec, at that time a placid little dude always smiling, would sit in a mainstream class without giving anyone a minute's trouble. He'd also not learn a thing.

Mainstream school might have been what I wanted, what I wished for, but it wasn't what he needed.

I'll admit that I had a little cry after I first looked around Alec's preferred special school. I'd never been around so many physically disabled kids before. Some of them needed wheelchairs, some were in stirrups, some even needed feeding apparatus.

Alec was walking unevenly, was still rather shaky and was in his own little world, but he didn't need any physical help. I found it scary. There was a small fear, a little voice inside that said, 'Is this where he fits in now? Is this the side of life that we're joining?'

Until then I'd had a really skewed image of the world, based on no understanding of disability whatsoever.

There was us 'normal' people over here in the happy corner. Then there were those poor, unfortunate disabled people in the sad corner. Crossing to their corner might mean that I'd catch being unhappy, so I ignored the other corner as much as possible. Fearful of it, I gave to charity, watched *Children in Need* and counted myself lucky.

Then – boom! – this was it, our new life, Alec's new life...in special school. For special people. Gulp.

I could see why parents did everything possible to keep their autistic children in mainstream schools, no matter what their suitability. This meant acknowledging that my pre-verbal child was not only different, but very, very different. In our own little family unit, we could choose what we wanted to believe. Here was the stark reality.

I didn't realise then that special schools are full of joy, love and laughter. They are filled to the brim with the warmest-hearted souls on earth.

Alec's school was perfect for him. Pretty soon I started to learn that the scary equipment bore little correlation with a child's mental abilities. Alec's schooling was tailored to his own needs, no one else's. Special schools don't work in bands or sets like mainstream ones do. They work according to style of learning.

Two assumptions that I'd made had been blown out of the water: first, that anyone who was severely physically disabled might be less mentally able than Alec and, second, that being put in a class of varying abilities would somehow drag him down.

Alec was put in the sensory class where he was encouraged to learn through engaging all his senses, through touch, vision and music. They used interactive white boards, which he loved. Pretty soon he started to blossom.

He had jobs, too. Responsibilities. At lunch, they sat him opposite kids who weren't keen on their food to show them how it was done. I couldn't believe it when they told me he took the register to the office. 'He doesn't always come straight back if there's something interesting going on in the hall,' smiled his teacher. 'But if it takes him a while, we send out a search party.'

Bobby stuck out like a sore thumb in mainstream. Flapping, humming, not saying much. Then he wrote all the letters of the alphabet in their correct order on the white board. He made a little friend. He had a teaching assistant who wasn't an expert in autism, but became an expert in him. He blossomed, too.

He was an orange alright, a confident one, a fun one. A quirky one. Who cared?

Positive thinking, I've found, is not some deluded state of mind. It's about getting real, tackling fear head on and taking a perspective that focuses on the £10,000 you've already won, not the £250,000 that you could have won.

After Alec's accident, I was grateful for every little thing. I was most grateful of all for the twins' happiness.

And then later I found that my kids thrived where others faltered, that there were umpteen cherries and sprinkles where at first all I saw was the Triad, that once I became used to this new way of living, it started to feel normal.

Autism was like a new pair of shoes. Once I'd walked in them a bit, they didn't feel so odd.

In our home, there's a little sign over the backdoor that my brother bought for me. It says, 'As far as anyone knows, we are a nice, normal family.'

I don't generally go for slogans in homes, being as they usually state the obvious. But I liked this one because it seemed almost ironic.

Despite the autism, we are still normal. Every family has their differences; ours just happens to be autism. We're not sitting in the unhappy corner, we're still here in the happy corner, where we belong. The autism is with us, part of us. It doesn't define us and we don't tell it what to do either, we just let it be.

We had made it through the diagnosis. But somewhere over the spectrum, there was a land that I hadn't even dreamed of when they were five years old – and step by step, I was heading further into my autism adventure.

5 If We Don't Fear the World, the World Won't Fear Us

Building a neurodiverse planet

Age ten, just asked Bobby why he insisted on bringing a bag of apples to school when there's a perfectly good tuckshop: 'Because I'm autistic, Mum. I do things MY way.'

Neurowhat?

Neurodiversity. It's a buzzword at the moment. In autism circles, you should drop it in every five sentences or so; you'll look as if you know what you're talking about.

Beneath the jargon, neurodiversity carries a very simple message and one that I've embraced wholeheartedly.

It means: we are all different and we should embrace this, rather than make everyone conform to the 'predominant neurotype'.

I swear to god they make up these phrases just so that they can run conferences.

Okay. Neurodiversity is more complicated than that. But you know what? To us parents that's about the size of it. From my viewpoint, it means living with what is and being happy with that.

I mention neurodiversity because if we want the world to accept autism and embrace those who are different, parents have an important role to play in making it happen. Essentially, this is because it means getting out there, getting the world used to 'different' and brushing off the pressure to conform when it comes to your child.

Easier said than done, I know. Ten years into this, I've just about got the hang of it.

Translated into my daily life, this now means trying my best not to tense up every time Alec is making a different noise or Bobby is flapping along the food aisle.

It means preparing the twins, which I'll be talking about in a later chapter. It means checking the timing is okay and that we're not putting ourselves under undue pressure. Until fairly recently, it meant having one person per twin in case one decided to go one way and the other in the opposite direction. These days, Bobby is fairly reliable and if he does disappear, he can usually be found with the console games.

My kids are different. And that's okay. Other people need to get used to that. Bobby and Alec can't pretend they don't have autism. They do, and the ironic thing is, the more tense I become about this, the more autistic their behaviour.

When my twins were younger and I was less thick-skinned, I regularly endured a floor-swallow-me-up feeling that was hard to shrug off with a smile.

I remember the time that I signed up my toddlers to Jo Jingles – a little music session where kids get to join in by shaking simple instruments. They both like music, I thought, this will be a great idea.

The kids all sat in a circle on their mums' laps, but Alec had other ideas. He stood in the middle of the gathering in his striped dungarees, bending in the middle so his head was upside down, then span a tambourine through his legs. It was pretty clever really, but it was hardly on the morning's agenda.

Then there was Harrison's birthday party. Bobby had yet to talk, but he had made a best friend at nursery, which just shows you how overrated talking is.

His non-autistic friend was called Harrison. Harrison wasn't even a nerd, he was really cool. They got on so well that Harrison invited Bobby to his fourth birthday party.

'Oh god,' I thought. 'Do we have to?'

I knew what would happen. Bobby would stick out like a sore thumb and I'd be left wondering which bits of autism I should explain and how I should go about doing that without making a big deal of it. You can't just drop, 'Sorry about that, he's got autism,' casually into the conversation without ensuring loads of follow-up well-meaning questions that you can't answer.

Then, of course, the conversational spotlight is on you. The discussion can't get beyond it. Instead of fitting in with the other parents, you're the odd one out, talking about your odd kid. And you know what? You may not be in the mood.

I was torn. The idea of a social invitation, when I'd specifically been told that my son was SOCIALLY IMPAIRED, was actually delightful. This was my autistic boy who was defying his diagnosis. Impaired shmimpaired. Ha ha.

Also, I felt that social skills practice would definitely be a plus and in fact I spent Bobby's early primary school years inviting half the class back after school and enthusiastically entertaining them while Bobby... Well, it wasn't that he was a bad host, he'd just sort of forgotten they were there.

Back to the party and, on the other hand, did I have the energy for what ensued?

Bobby, dressed in his best shirt, arrived at Harrison's house and found a spinning top. Pretty much instantly, the rest of the world had melted away while he focused on it. Then he decided to explore the rooms that he wasn't supposed to go in. As for pass the parcel... Pass the what? I am supposed to do *what* with it? Oh no. No thank you.

We didn't even begin to attempt musical statues.

I saw Harrison's bemused face and I could tell what he was thinking. How could Bobby, so much fun, so relaxed at nursery, turn overnight into this frankly weird kid he didn't recognise?

Bobby was out of his comfort zone, that's how come.

If we're following the Autism Sundae Dessert analogy, because of unfamiliar surroundings, his chocolate scoop (problems with communication) and his vanilla scoop (social interaction) had just doubled in size.

This was caused by the presence of the third strawberry scoop – lack of flexibility. His brain just couldn't generalise enough to recognise that a new situation carried certain familiar factors. He was tense, and tension showed itself in repetitive behaviour.

I explained to some understanding parents that Bobby had autism and we returned home unscathed. Well, Bobby did; my pride had certainly taken a bashing.

This kind of thing happened again and again… and again.

But the more we did this, the easier it became. By the age of seven, Bobby had been to enough birthday parties that he had learnt what to do. As I'll keep saying in this book until you are bored to tears, what they didn't learn automatically, they learnt through experience.

I never turned an invitation down, even though as the years went by I became the mum who stayed long after other parents had left their excitable children with the host and headed off smugly to a nearby pub.

I never turned an invitation down, because I didn't want Bobby to be the one who earned a reputation as the kid who didn't 'do' social outings.

When Bobby was seven, he attended a friend's party at a social club and, while I was there, I took the sort of photograph that only a parent of a child with autism would take.

It's not very clear, but it shows children sitting in a circle and sitting with them is Bobby. Bobby is PASSING THE ACTUAL PARCEL!

In that moment, my heart brimmed with pride.

Experience taught him to do what other kids knew naturally. Experience also taught Bobby that most things follow a pattern. You go to a party, you stuff your face with cake, you play pass the parcel, you come home with a prize you don't want and you give it to Alec. Everyone got used to him wearing headphones to protect himself from the noise and Bobby became more adaptable.

And gradually Bobby's world got bigger.

I learnt to ask myself this question: am I wanting to avoid this situation for him or me?

If the answer was for him, because it would make him stressed, then fair enough. If the answer was, 'For me, because I don't like my kid looking weird,' then I realised I was going to have to swallow that for Bobby's sake. The more I avoided social situations, the weirder Bobby was going to be once in them.

Besides, just because he didn't have any idea how to play musical statues, it didn't mean that he wasn't enjoying himself.

Aged six, Alec had a great time at a sea-lion show at Knowsley Safari Park. He spent the entire time watching a large fan high up in the corner of the room, ignoring the seal balancing a ball on its nose. When you pay for a ticket, you can't really tell what they're going to get out of the experience.

Eventually, I left Bobby at a party at about the age of nine with a mum who had her head screwed on. I came back a couple of hours later with my shoulders up to nose-height in tense expectation. He'd been fine.

These days, as long as I know the people well, I can leave him at someone else's house no problem. If he's with a friend, they tend to be relaxed, playing video games.

Occasionally, I've been a bit too relaxed and eased off the reins a bit too much. When Bobby made a friend at a holiday club and she invited him round to her house, I decided for once to drop all explanations about autism. He was by now about 11. I figured they'd be in the house playing, what could go wrong?

What went wrong was that her mum took the daughter, siblings and Bobby on a long walk. Bobby doesn't do long walks. He tripped over and broke a little glass ring that he'd been carrying for his new friend.

Then he had a meltdown.

Her mum hadn't seen a meltdown of this scale before and I don't think she ever wants to see one again.

It was my fault. There is a thin line to tread between giving a new friend's mum an entire guidebook and not arming them with enough information on autism to know the basics. For once, over-confident, I'd slipped off that thin line and it took his little friend a while to recover. She didn't get in touch for a bit, but, to give her credit, she is still friendly with him.

And Alec?

He was never that interested in other kids. Alec was on a different pathway and our main focus was helping him to tolerate new adults, which he did admirably, and play alongside other children.

He had joint birthday parties with his twin, but no one kidded themselves that it wasn't all about the cake.

The one thing you could rely on with Alec was that in any social situation, no matter how outside his comfort zone he was, he could always eat. If you kept the food coming, you stood a good chance of making it through the afternoon without fuss.

He once got through an entire wedding on a giant packet of Haribo sweets.

There were times that I put myself through unnecessary stress just to make a point to myself that normal life was going to be lived.

This included going to see Father Christmas when they were ten, even though Alec hadn't got a clue who Father Christmas was. Let's face it, the concept of an old guy with a white beard who squeezes down a chimney to give you presents isn't an easy one to swallow at the best of times.

Until then, we'd avoided trips to Father Christmas. They hadn't really got it. They did now (well, Bobby did) and I wanted them to see the big guy before they were too big for it themselves. Alec was already twice the size of most kids his age anyway. One of the mums used to ask if I put him in a growbag at night.

I was with Tori and we rocked up at Manchester's immense shopping palace, the Trafford Centre, hoping for a delightful, lit-up grotto.

If Alec doesn't know who Father Christmas is, he certainly appreciates the twinkling glitter and glamour of the festive season.

I spend each year adorning our Christmas tree with tasteful decorations. I never learn; I take ages over it. Alec then spends each year denuding the Christmas tree of baubles. What starts off as a delicately choreographed arrangement ends up looking like I did it with my eyes closed in a hailstorm.

Last year, I hung up a series of transparent baubles filled with tiny foil stars. I later found Alec watching TV, munching the stars from his hand, the empty bauble lying close by.

'No, Alec, not good for you! Tummy ache!' I indicated by groaning and rubbing my stomach.

Alec looked as if he didn't mind the tummy ache, although the stars weren't very flavoursome. He has the constitution of an ox, which is just as well, considering the number of unusual things that have made it through his alimentary canal.

Snow is Alec's favourite thing on earth. He loves ice. He loves the look of it, the feel of it and most of all the crunch of it. He can munch his way through a glass of ice cubes no problem, without any sign of brain freeze. We are talking a cheap date, here.

We have some difficulty when it comes to snow. Alec doesn't really notice the difference between the clean stuff that it's okay to eat and the stuff that still has gravel in it.

In the case of our Trafford Centre visit to Father Christmas, he had yet to recognise that the grotto was covered in fake snow and disappointedly tugged away at some fluffy stuff. He was also making some excited squealy noises that took a few little kids by surprise.

There weren't nearly enough sparkly bits to keep him amused.

With all my brashness, I was starting to feel this was a bad idea.

We were then obliged to watch some short Christmas cartoon, which was the longest ten minutes of my life.

Boy, these places know how to drag out a very basic task. Sometimes they do allow you to skip these bits, so it's always worth asking beforehand if there is any time-wasting crap that they have to sit through. Although maybe don't phrase it quite like that on the phone.

Eventually, we were taken to see Father Christmas along a corridor that had a lot of curtains. Curious as ever, Alec peeked behind one of them and made an elf gasp. He wasn't supposed to know that there was more than one Santa here. Not that he could report this to anyone and not that he even cared or minded. I was faintly amused to register the shock on the elf's face though. It was as if in one gesture Alec had single-handedly wrecked Christmas.

We got to Father Christmas and I had to explain that the twins had autism, otherwise he would have been confused that the conversation was limited to Pokémon. They had to pose for a picture and Alec wouldn't stand on the right spot.

'Act normal. Please. For once in your lives,' I thought. 'Just do me this total favour of smiling, both at once for the camera with Father Christmas. Give me a photograph I can put on Facebook.'

Bobby gave his cheesiest posed grin, the one that I tend to ban. On the third attempt, Alec sort of looked at the camera. Father Christmas tried his best, being as these days they aren't allowed to hold the kids close.

We left with presents that neither of the kids wanted.

The huge irony of going out with your autistic children is this: the more you want – no, pray – for them to ACT

NORMAL and do what everyone else is doing, the less likely that is to happen.

The tenser you are about the situation, the more they pick up on it and the anxiety starts to influence their behaviour.

Autistic kids are like emotional sponges. I've especially found this with Alec. Some days, I'll be thinking, 'Why is he in such a mood?' Then it will dawn on me that it's because I'm in one.

> The huge irony of going out with your autistic children is this: the more you want – no, pray – for them to ACT NORMAL and do what everyone else is doing, the less likely that is to happen.

Want them to act 'normal'? Take them to an inclusive, accepting environment where people understand autism and there's no social pressure on them. Kick off your heels and watch the most settled behaviour you've seen all year.

Want them to be at their most autistic? Ramp the pressure up, tense up and give them a list of things they shouldn't be doing.

I have an adult example of this in Tim, who works in *AuKids'* office. When you put Tim outside an environment he is comfortable in, you'll get a lot of nervous gestures and he can barely make conversation. Once inside the *AuKids'* office, where everyone accepts autism and knows him, you get a different person – an articulate, bright, happy, focused person.

I can see a better future where everyone accepts the concept of neurodiversity, but it's going to take a combination of two factors. One is parents not shying away or getting embarrassed because their children are different. The other is a result of that: people learning to recognise, accept and live with difference.

These days, Alec is on a personal mission to get everyone to accept different, with regular outings to B&Q (his dad's favourite hardware store). He loves the high warehouse ceilings and the wide aisles, and he happily yodels along with them at top volume while Gavin seeks that elusive little nut, bolt, piece of wood, piping, lightbulb, cable or other little widget.

Alec's alternative noises sometimes make people look up from what they are doing. And then they see Gavin's relaxed body language, his smile and Alec's happy deportment. They figure this is quite normal for us and they carry on with what they are doing.

Yep, that's right. They carry on with what they are doing. Looking up to register a noise that wasn't quite what they expected has taken them a whole six seconds. It hasn't harmed them or interrupted them.

The 'looks' that can make you feel a bit sensitive are normal. The human brain is programmed to

. . . .

I can see a better future where everyone accepts the concept of neurodiversity, but it's going to take parents not getting embarrassed by their children's differences and others learning to recognise, accept and live with difference.

. . . .

respond to a new noise in case it's a warning of danger. That means that people will look up when they see Alec. Then they carry on.

I'd also like to make it clear here that anyone who presumes to comment on another child's behaviour is a waste of space, anyway. I'm not going to restrict my life just because of a small bunch of narrow-minded people who aren't worth my anxiety.

For a start, there is too much at stake. If people don't see others with autism in public places, then a world that's in tune with neurodiversity won't happen.

If we get embarrassed about our kids and 'shush' them in places where it's not critical that they're quiet, we send everyone else a big message. What we're telling them is that autism is unacceptable or not okay.

There's something even worse than that: we're sending our kids the same message.

When I think about what's appropriate and what's not appropriate, and teaching them behaviour that's acceptable in public, I'm conscious that I don't want them to hurt others, or break things, or walk away without paying. But these days, if they're a bit noisy or unusual, I do honestly think, 'So what?'

Gav's better at this than I am. He not only thinks, 'So what?', he gets a kick out of the little surprises that Alec causes people. He likes to jerk people out of their comfort zones.

I'm sure relaxing about the autism in public has had a big knock-on effect on how the twins feel about themselves.

Our friend Tim grew up at about the same time as me, in an age where not very much was known about autism.

But his mum seemed to instinctively catch on to one thing: if she wanted her son to have a life, he had to get out there.

Get out there he did, eventually getting a job with us. Tim was taught from an early age that despite the impact that autism had on him, he shouldn't let it stand in his way or be ashamed of it.

Now Tim not only has a full and rewarding life, but he also delivers talks about autism. He has become the magazine's autism advocate.

His mum's bravery and her merry indifference to an intolerant world led to Tim educating others in what it feels like to be him, leading to more acceptance and understanding.

I'm giving it a go. I've got used to us being a bit different in public. Yesterday, Bobby accompanied me to the clothes shops, Pikachu under his arm. He occasionally walked backwards and forwards in a mini ritual. He said hello to a few people when, strictly speaking, he should have ignored them. They were okay with it, though, even though I told him afterwards why that wasn't such a great idea.

We don't talk to strangers. Non-autistic people aren't that friendly (I didn't actually say that, but I thought it).

I have learnt over the years that despite me being very aware of the twins' differences, other people aren't really looking at us funny.

And if anyone is, they need a hobby.

6 Learning Aut-Speak

Understanding echolalia

Age ten: 'Bobby, your hairdresser phoned up today to say she had found a Mario Kart DS game by reception and was it yours? Wasn't that kind of her? Look after your things!'

'Oh MAN, I am in BIG TROUBLE YOUNG MAN.'

When it comes to talking, we speak two languages at home: English and Aut-speak.

Well actually, we speak English and we *understand* Aut-speak. The main difference between other types of language and Aut-speak is that other types of language are spoken like a ball game, whereas in Aut-speak, you have to kind of snatch the ball for a bit.

For Bobby, language processing is tough. Our language moves at an incredible speed and is full of new ideas, inflections, tone and nuance.

Even though he can now talk (having developed speech late at the age of nearly four), and despite his intelligence, listening to language at other people's pace is a bit like trying to play Grade 8 music when you've only just mastered Grade 4.

It takes a lot out of him.

So, what Bobby does is what most other people on the spectrum do for escape, comfort and relaxation. He keeps himself company with Aut-speak.

This is Bobby's inner language, but worn on the outside so that others can hear it.

Having a conversation all on your own may not be that recognisable socially, but it sure saves the hassle of the processing required for a two-way dialogue.

So, yup, your kid is sounding weird in public and he won't change it because he doesn't care. I've got used to this, but I have made him aware of the volume of his voice, with a scale of 1–5. Volume 1 is a whisper and Volume 5 is shouting your head off.

In primary school assemblies, Bobby was reminded to use Volume 1 and would carry a picture of a mouse to remind himself to be as quiet as one. This made no difference whatsoever when it came to headteacher Mr Cunningham's rhetorical questions, which Bobby felt obliged to answer loudly on everyone else's behalf.

The brilliant thing about Outwood Primary School was that no one minded. In fact, they liked it.

A scoring method like the volume one saves the trouble of someone with autism having to interpret vague social etiquette and works really well for all sorts of things, because it gives them an easy rule of thumb.

There's a fantastic book on this called *The Incredible 5-Point Scale* (Dunn Buron and Curtis 2012), which I often recommend.

When Aut-speak takes the form of a repetitious monologue or repeated phrases, it's called echolalia.

I think of echolalia as a kind of entertainment for autistic people, but it can also be a great comfort.

If you think it sounds weird, just imagine what you'd be saying to yourself if someone asked you to abseil down the side of a building.

I wouldn't be surprised if, as you make your way over the edge of that building, your fingers grasping the rope and your knuckles white, you're saying out loud, 'You're okay, you're okay, you're okay, you can do this, you can do this, you can do this.'

We all repeat things to ourselves when put under stress. It's just that, for autistic people, coping with everyday life can seem like climbing over the edge of a building. There is so much unexpected and their brains simply aren't built to cope with uncertainty.

In an uncertain world, where processing social dialogue is difficult and even small environmental changes can feel like an attack, this internal comfort chatter, Aut-speak, seems to be a fantastic inner resource.

I've called it Aut-speak rather than echolalia for two reasons. First, it's because I hate technical speak when we're talking about real, cuddly people. Second, it's because echolalia implies (to me, anyway) that the language is just a verbal echo, empty of meaning.

When Bobby talks in this way, he is constantly reliving emotional highlights – he creates for himself entire imaginary landscapes through repetition.

The commentary on a Super Mario arcade game, a series of YouTube clips, snippets of a film or a TV programme...all of them are stored in a substantial mental folder to be recalled at will. He uses echolalia when he's unsure about his surroundings, when he's nervous, when he's a bit bored and when...oh, just because, 'Solitude is as needful to the imagination as society is wholesome for the character,' as said by James Russell Lowell the 19th-century American poet.

His amazing memory is partly the result of Bobby's capacity to listen to the same things many more times than a non-autistic person would be able to tolerate. Having no boredom switch can be a good thing. With such accurate recall, he has access to his own mental DVD catalogue.

The repetition isn't just for comfort, though. I've seen Bobby in mid-patter and quite frankly he's being his own superb company – he just delights himself.

Parents can get concerned about echolalia because it doesn't appear to be meaningful language.

Personally, I'm not concerned about it at all. I've seen it help Bobby's language development by enabling him to express difficult emotions and I think it's a great coping mechanism.

When he was younger, Bobby would use a 'cut-and-paste' form of repetition to indicate what he was experiencing.

When he got stressed, he'd shout, 'I'M LOST, ANDY IS GONE!', which you'll probably recognise as the scene in *Toy Story* when Woody and Buzz find themselves abandoned in a gas station.

This ready-made dialogue was fast-food language for when his emotions overtook him. When that happened, his limited expression, which was difficult for him at the best of times, became even more constrained.

It was a slightly inaccurate gluing job, but it was effective.

Sometimes, even now, we'll be in the middle of a conversation when it swaps between English and Aut-speak quite suddenly.

I said something Bobby didn't agree with the other day and his response was, 'You're stressing me out and now I have a superpower to kill you with lightning!'

I didn't take offence – this was a 'cut and paste' from a Mario Kart racing game. Well, er, I hope it was.

If you hear what your child is hearing and look at what they're looking at, you start to realise that they're not bonkers with language, they're simply *borrowers* of language.

When he's not under stress, the cut-and-paste sections of Bobby's conversation are quite smooth and it's only really when you know him well (or you know his favourite YouTubers) that you can hear the join.

So, Aut-speak has many purposes. It comforts, it relaxes, it helps with language familiarisation and it's very expressive when needed.

It's also the best self-entertainment system ever. If you're autistic, you're lucky

> **If you hear what your child is hearing and look at what they're looking at, you start to realise that they're not bonkers with language, they're simply *borrowers* of language.**

enough to be endlessly excited and amused by the same thought.

Wow.

Before you call anyone lonely, check to see if they have a vibrant inner life that most of us can only imagine.

Bobby loves company…but he enjoys his own the best.

7 Specialisms Make Specialists

Valuing special interests

I found a great way of getting rid of sales calls at home. I get Bobby to answer the phone any time the display says 'Out of Area' and tell him he can talk about meerkats as much as he likes.

We act as though comfort and luxury were the chief requirements of life, when all we need to make us really happy is something to be enthusiastic about.

Charles Kingsley

The most noticeable aspect of Aut-speak is when people talk about the same thing for a long time.

These keen interests are sometimes called 'obsessions', which is another judgemental term used by non-autistics. It's one we don't need if we're living in a neurodiverse world, thanks very much.

Some people call them special interests. I just call them 'specialisms'.

When speaking about their specialist subject, an autistic child may genuinely not realise you've been temporarily replaced with a glazed-looking fish.

Why don't they twig? The visual part of their brain doesn't chat to the social–emotional side very well (if you want to know more about this, read Peter Vermeulen's terrific book *Autism as Context Blindness* (Vermeulen 2012)).

I call it joining the dots. They may be able to recognise a bored face, but it will not occur that the source of the boredom was that they'd become a keynote speaker on Duracell batteries when you didn't actually sign up for the Duracell conference in the first place.

The closest I get in my world to Aut-speak is when I develop a passion for a particular song on a new album.

I know I should be listening to the entire album from start to finish, but I can't help fast-forwarding to Track 8. It jangles round my head, day after day. Sometimes I love this; sometimes the inescapable nature of this momentary addiction bugs me. Music is one of the few things in my life that has the capacity to be inescapable.

When Bobby and Alec like something, the same thing happens. The main difference is that whereas I can keep the incessant little melody inside my head, Bobby can't do this with words. He is compelled to say them instead – and he really doesn't care what this looks or sounds like to anyone else.

Really, this kind of passion is lovely. Yet social skills have to be learnt and so our kids are gradually taught to realise that there's a time and place to talk about Pokémon or GoAnimate clips (his latest).

To help Bobby realise when he was getting carried away with his specialisms, we developed the idea of Listening Patience.

I explained that everyone has Listening Patience for about two minutes. That's the length of time they can listen without taking part in a conversation before they start to get bored.

It's a bit rough and ready of course, and I realise it's not true for every situation, but in Bobby's case and with the sort of conversations he has, it was a crude way of getting the concept of turn-taking across.

You can be quite direct to autistic people without causing offence and so a small reminder about Listening Patience worked very well.

Then, one day when I was telling him off, he told me he'd run out of Listening Patience.

Touché.

Teaching him about Listening Patience means that Bobby's Aut-speak is beginning to turn into a two-way conversation when it comes to specialisms. He also saves most of these chats for his autistic mates, who share a lot of the same interests and can give far better feedback than I can. It is actually not much fun talking about a specialism to someone like me who asks silly questions all the time.

I know some books suggest that you make diary time for a person to talk about a specialism. I don't really agree with that. It's a completely artificial technique of conversing. If a specialism is what you want to talk about then fine, talk about it, but you may need to learn a little about how your information is being received and how to make it easier to listen to. Specialisms are great training ground for conversation skills, so don't knock them.

The big irony of autism parenting is that you spend years wishing – no, praying – your child will talk. Then, suddenly, they do talk. They are talking about something they like in minute detail. Every day. For hours.

Having wished that they would start to talk, you can't help but have moments when you wish just as fervently they would give it a rest.

I am not being unkind here. This is the reality of living with someone whose mental pathways tend to lead to the same place. You can love them and yet be sick to the gills of Pokémon at the same time; it's possible. It's not denying your love for your child to admit it.

However, I do think autistic people can give us all a valuable lesson here. As a society, we're pretty lame at being interested in anything other than other people – you only have to look at the magazine shelves to see how much we enjoy reading about other people's lives.

Sometimes the autistic fascination with things – with facts, with knowledge and with statistics – does make for deeper, more enriching company. That is, it does as long as they can get hold of that Listening Patience idea and bear in mind that we all have shorter attention spans than them.

In a presentation that has stayed with me forever, autistic speaker Ros Blackburn said, 'Non-autistic people DO have obsessions – other people!' (Blackburn 2011).

Specialisms turn people into specialists. This focus can lead to brilliance.

It's unfortunate that people who have 'obsessions' about *things* are sometimes dubbed 'weird' or a 'nerd' by their peers.

When a person's obsession leads to great achievement, we conveniently forget that we called them a nerd and we turn their lives into a film starring Russell Crowe.

Specialisms turn people into specialists. This focus can lead to brilliance.

> Men give me credit for some genius. All the genius I have is this; when I have a subject in mind, I study it profoundly. Day and night, it is before me. My mind becomes pervaded with it…the effort which I have made is what people are pleased to call genius. It is the fruit of labour and thought. (American statesman Alexander Hamilton)

The ability to focus on one thing is admirable and, although not unique to the autistic brain, it is certainly one of the positive aspects of being on the spectrum.

Self-confidence and inner happiness give you the resources to meet with the peculiar non-autistic world and let it in.

Self-confidence (from having your own interests valued) and inner happiness (through the escape of specialisms) give you the resources to meet with the peculiar non-autistic world and let it in.

So, value the nerdy part of autism. It's so much better for them than constantly tripping up over their social shoelaces to try to restrain who they really are.

That's not to say that there isn't a time and place. That's where teaching social skills come in handy.

As parents, we don't sit down and train social skills at the dining room table. It happens everywhere.

Like in a traffic jam.

At 3.15pm, it's school collecting time and Aut-speak starts pretty much the minute Bobby hops in the car.

'How was your day?' he asks. He has learnt to ask this. It's brilliant that he does it.

'Mine was good thanks, how was yours?'

'My day was awesome!' reports Bobby.

With its constant flurry of social exchanges, its noise, changes and demands, secondary school is hardly a relaxing place for a pupil with autism. To survive it is indeed AWESOME.

But we're not talking about school. We're talking about Pokémon news.

'The Pokémon generation two update is arriving in three days' time! Did you know that, Mum?'

'Wow, that's exciting.' I do know that, because he told me a fortnight ago, then a week ago and then every day until today.

It's still good that he asked me if I knew. What used to be a monologue is now a conversation.

Bobby has learnt, through our discussions on his specialisms, to check my understanding. As long as he reminds himself that I am a listener, he has fulfilled his side of the bargain.

While Bobby logs in to Pokémon Go on his iPad, I steer the car around approximately a thousand teenagers with no road sense. Or maybe they have road sense but they're too arrogant to use it. They amble ludicrously among the cars that are already having enough of a problem negotiating each other through the narrow school street.

If I'm lucky, a school coach adds to the confusion. A triad of testosterone-fuelled lads swim among the cars on bicycles, standing up in their seats. While I'm admiring of any teen who can master a two-wheeler this well (Bobby and Alec never could), I'm also concentrating quite hard on not killing them.

'Mum. Mum! Did you know about Pokémon second generation?'

'Er Bobby, remember bad times and good times? Now is not a good time...'

As I mentioned before, we have practised social situations as if each were a Lego® kit. Each is dissected into its component pieces and, with detailed explanation, put back together to build an understanding of acceptable behaviour. In this case, 'The Best Time to Ask A Question' was a Social Story™ I developed for Bobby after it became clear that he wasn't picking up 'busy' signals and was therefore far less likely to get what he wanted.

Social Stories are little preparation guides made in a certain format for the purpose of filling in gaps for your child so that they know the best way to tackle social situations. I'll tell you more about them later.

'Oh yeh – sorry about that.'

'It's okay, Bobby, once I've got past this traffic I will be able to concentrate much better and then I will be a better listener.'

I have learnt to explain what I'm thinking, brick by brick.

I've got to the traffic lights where the weary teachers are out on patrol, checking that their young students make it on to the bus in one piece. And off we drive to Alec's school, where my language will change from Aut-speak to Alecish.

8 Communication Is What Happens While You're Waiting for Speech

Parenting a non-verbal child

Reading a story to Bobby, age nine, I commented that it was a darn clever horse that could talk. Bobby replied: 'Yeh, he's SO darn.'

I peer through the assembly-hall window and wave at Alec. He is not usually looking at me but has some sort of sixth sense alerting him to my arrival.

A lopsided grin (a vestige of his accident) emerges and he lollops towards me. Alec had to learn to walk again and his gait is quite uneven, but he makes it about pretty fast.

Once face to face with me – there is no polite distance – he is already placing wet kisses minus any decent suction on to my cheek and, although I'm happy to see him, I have to prise his fingers off my neck because social skills training is a 24/7 job.

Alec is now as tall as me and his cuddles are more like being mugged. In a nice way, of course. I immediately start to speak Alecish.

'Gentle Alec – gentle!'

Gentle is for saps. He gives a little whoop and heads for the door. If you imagine R2-D2's speech, Alecish isn't far from that, with some added Tarzan-style yodels. The words are all in his head, but his brain scrambles them before they get out. As Bobby once said, 'Alec's speech is broken so he can't use it.'

I know pretty much exactly what Alec is thinking through signs, pictures, gestures, movements, gaze and a wealth of other signals. I can tell what he's thinking, but I can't tell what he's experiencing.

I know it's nothing like what I experience, and that bugs the hell out of me. It's like being given a secret diary with a padlock on it.

I try to put on the car radio, but Alec points from the back seat. This means, 'Switch it off, you are distracting me,' indicating how sensitive his hearing is. Although I don't know what he's experiencing, if I pay close attention to his behaviour, I can have a pretty good guess.

I switch it off. In any case, nothing can compete with Bobby's Pokémon Go theme.

In the back of the car Alec is busy sorting out his cordless headphones. He has broken about three jacks when they were irretrievably lodged inside his iPad socket. His new Bluetooth headphones spare us a lot of torment, partially because they don't have a jack but mainly because we no longer have to listen to a lot of repetition. Alec likes to hear a particular line from the song 'Don't Look Back in Anger' 40 times over.

This is Alec's form of echolalia. While he can't speak repetitively, we can tell that his thoughts are repetitive because of the amount he listens to the same thing.

He divides music and videos up into very small loops and repeats them for himself. It's as if he cannot process it all in one chunk.

This way of processing new information is recognisable in Bobby's behaviour, too. He won't wear a new piece of clothing straight away, he'll get used to it in his wardrobe first. If someone gives him an exciting present, he'll look disinterested to start (with relatives trying not to look aggrieved).

It's not that he doesn't like it, he just needs time for it to 'bed in', for the new information to be welcomed to headquarters.

Alec hasn't got the Bluetooth connection going yet and as we drive up Buckingham Road West I'm starting to grit my teeth slightly.

I'm an Oasis fan as much as the next one, but if I hear 'So Sally can wait...' more than five times, I start to think, 'No she can't wait. She needs to get a bloody move on.'

Parenting a non-verbal child is exceptionally hard work, don't let anyone tell you otherwise. Ahead of all your other parenting priorities, you have an extra layer. Your job is to ensure that your child somehow has the means to communicate.

But before that, you have to learn a very important lesson about autism, and this is that your child may not understand the purpose of communication. It's caused by not realising that their thoughts differ from yours.

Understanding this about Alec and Bobby was quite major for me. Until then, I'd assumed that they didn't speak because of some physical difficulty. I didn't know what speech and language therapy was for, but I imagined that it was a case of magically conjuring words out of the twins through some mystical power that I didn't possess.

I had no idea that when it comes to autism, much of speech and language therapy is to do with helping autistic kids to understand that communication GETS YOU STUFF.

And guess what? Once you've learnt how to motivate them, and how to build on what's emerging, you can work on it yourself.

I was very fortunate in meeting speech and language therapist, Tori Houghton, just six months after my twins were diagnosed with autism.

Tori was part of a team working on a new study run by Manchester University called PACT (Pre-school Autism Communication Trial). She used PACT therapy with our family even though we weren't part of the research.

PACT used a range of familiar speech and language therapy approaches to nurture parent–child communication, but its real difference was in training parents in observation techniques and allowing them to recognise their own successes and build on them through a combination of video footage and careful questioning from the speech and language therapist.

During a session, a parent was videoed for ten minutes playing with their child. The parent and therapist then watched it back together, with the therapist encouraging the parent to watch for positive interactions, enjoyable moments and communication signals.

The basis of the approach was to help parents identify key moments when language and communication were happening and to be able to capitalise on them in future interactions at home. What they'd learnt could be beautifully transferred.

Using this technique, parents could be trained to become communication experts with their own child. This not only improved communication between parent and child – it also brought parents generally closer to their children as they formed the confidence to read them successfully.

This underlying message that parents shouldn't have to hand over their children to experts to improve their chances really resonated with me.

Tori and I had a joint appreciation for this approach and it later formed the foundation for *AuKids* magazine. The idea that parents learn better by drawing on their expert knowledge of their own child, rather than listening for one-size-fits-all instructions from an authority figure was extended to our magazine's content and style.

The most significant result of PACT was that the parents engaging in the therapy were more in tune with their children, shown by increased interaction.

What was particularly unusual – and what made the headlines – was that these changes were sustained in the follow-up study six years later. This had been difficult to achieve previously and shows that early intervention using parents can have lasting effects.

It didn't take the follow-up study for me to be convinced about PACT techniques. Training me up to take command of the job that I did daily just seemed logical. I didn't want to be a helpless, angry parent jumping up and down telling everyone that my child didn't get enough hours of speech therapy. If I could learn how to interact with Alec myself – and pass that on to others who knew him – then bring it on!

I saw the results for myself. Through this, I learnt to interact successfully with both Bobby and Alec.

Until I met Tori, I'd been finding Alec very hard to play with. He seemed to ignore me completely. Try as I might to join in with his play, he remained in his own world.

It's hard to be around a child who doesn't give any feedback. I mean, not just a bit hard, but desperately hard. It wasn't just hard for us, it was sad for Alec's extended family, too.

In all the literature I've read, I've never once come across anything that acknowledges what a profound effect this lack of connection can have on our happiness and confidence as parents.

To tease out the tiniest bit of feedback, we become more animated, ask questions, place demands – in short, exactly what they DON'T need!

After every failed attempt, your shoulders sag and you feel an extra little tug of despair.

To tease out the tiniest bit of feedback, we become more animated, ask questions, place demands – in short, exactly what they DON'T need!

But does anyone tell us this? Nope.

Eventually, after experiencing rejection from their youngsters numerous times, some parents give up.

They think, 'This is autism. That's just what my child's like. They cannot connect.'

You can't really blame them.

Yet, although they may not be able to show it, our kids do sense that rejection. And they CAN connect – they just cannot tell us what they need.

I learnt this just by watching back a few films of myself and the twins. These were my lightbulb moments and had a huge effect on me.

When Tori and I reviewed our films of Alec and I, we paused certain key moments. It struck me like a bolt of lightning that my anxiety at Alec's lack of speech was translating into my behaviour with him.

In response to his passiveness, I was lively and exuberant. In response to his lack of rapport, I was pushing ever more exciting things under his face. 'Look at this!' 'See what this does!' 'This is BRILLIANT!'

I think a lot of parents have a similar experience. There's one thought that jabs away at us: *My kid doesn't like me. If he liked me, he'd look up and smile. He'd respond.*

So, we try extra hard, but what we are doing drives them even further away.

Alec was usually very cuddly. But he moved away every time I came near him to play. Looking at the video, I cringed as I saw him twist his entire body to face the opposite direction.

Unfortunately, some parents don't get much further than that. Desperate and hopeless, unable to spend any rewarding time together, they hire other people to spend time with their children instead. They miss out on a bond that they think they're unworthy of having.

When I watched that video with Tori, I clearly saw Alec getting overwhelmed by me. I was too 'in his face', too loud, too demanding. He couldn't meet my demands, so he withdrew. He was experiencing overload, and I had interpreted his passiveness as disinterest and, worse, a lack of love.

Your kid loves you. Take it from me, children want to love their parents and they want to be loved. But autism means that they won't necessarily fling their arms around you or beam at you the minute you walk through the door.

As parents, we have to rise above this and not interpret it as rejection.

During the next speech and language therapy session, I changed my behaviour. I found that if I just watched him, Alec was happy for me to be there. He even began to pass me things.

The irony wasn't lost on me that speech and language therapy in my case meant shutting up. The speech and language therapy wasn't really for him, it was for me. I was the one who needed to adapt. Who knew?

Once I had learnt to keep a polite distance from Alec and join in with what he was doing rather than impose my own agenda on him, he became a lot happier. I followed Alec's focus – even if he was just spinning a toy helicopter blade – and supplied the odd word for him, based on what he was watching.

This is something that's called shared interaction in speech and language therapy circles, and it involves responding to the child's thoughts and feelings as well as experiences. It isn't simply copying but becoming more in tune with intentions, creating better communication.

What I learnt through PACT is that you can only have a proper conversation once you learn to translate non-verbal signals.

I learnt to be with Alec without making lots of language demands.

It turns out that when your language processing is slow, less is a whole lot more.

Alec had been sending signals in neon lights, but I'd missed them.

What I learnt through PACT is that you can only have a proper conversation once you learn to translate non-verbal signals.

Only then can you become part of the conversation that your child is having with themselves. Communication expert Phoebe Caldwell described a child's interaction with themselves as an uninterrupted loop. By engaging with them at a level they can process, you become part of that loop and the conversation can become two-way, even if it's in gestures and not speech (Caldwell 2015).

After these sessions, I started to recognise when Alec was trying to speak to me without words.

After PACT therapy established the beginnings of interaction, we were able to build on Alec's language skills in different ways. He was now not far off getting his point across using symbols and signs.

With Bobby, this kind of interaction built up his vocabulary and his trust. He wasn't experiencing overload but his processing was delayed, something I picked up when I watched back a video and saw that he had actually copied me in his play, but some minutes later than you'd expect.

If you're ever wondering why autism parents are so highly attuned to other people's feelings, it's because they're used to watching non-verbals like a hawk.

This includes the sorts of signals that will give you clues about what a child's sensory experience of the world is like. Sadly, I can't walk around Alec's head. But my three favourite books on this subject – Olga Bogdashina's *Sensory Perceptual Issues in Autism* (2016), Rachel Schneider's *Making Sense: A Guide to Sensory Issues* (2016) and Phoebe Caldwell's *The Anger Box* (2014b) – have trained me in what to look out for.

Alec prefers listening and touching things than looking at them, which tells me he trusts these senses more than his sight. His sight is perfectly fine, but his visual perception is unreliable.

Alec likes to wear ear defenders. For a long time, I did wonder if this was just down to sensitive hearing. I'm now convinced that dampening down the volume is the easiest and quickest way Alec can cut down on massive general sensory overload. I can't be sure, though.

The fact that Alec twiddles a piece of string whenever he gets the chance also shows me that he gets overloaded very quickly and has to focus intensely on something familiar – it blocks out everything else. So, although he doesn't seem to be screaming at his environment, he is quietly shutting himself off from it.

Something else that I wasn't told early enough is that you can't label your child over-sensitive in one sensory area and under-sensitive in another. It doesn't always work that way. What makes Alec more difficult to interpret is that I'm aware that one day he could be over-sensitive to some form of sensory input and, another day, he could be under-sensitive to the same thing.

It's autistic people themselves who have taught us this with their powerful accounts of living with SPD (another piece of jargon – Sensory Processing Disorder).

Some days, I see that Alec is clear and focused and it's as if the clouds have parted. I imagine those are the days where his sensory difficulties are getting in the way less. Difficulties vary daily and are also linked to the stress of his surroundings. Many people report sensory difficulties increasing in severity when they are stressed.

Once Alec realised that I was a reliable communicator, that he could send me messages and it would GET HIM STUFF, we worked on techniques that would act as alternatives to verbal language. We started with symbols and later adopted sign language, too.

Waiting for speech to arrive is a bit like waiting for a very, very late bus. Do I give up on the bus and start walking to my destination? Or do I stand here waiting patiently while everything else is delayed as a result?

It's hard to keep faith by working on symbols and signs when hope is always there that speech may develop.

But what if you knew that working on those alternatives is MORE LIKELY to make the bus arrive?

Parents just aren't told this.

You might well adopt the 'wait and see' method, thinking that anything other than speech is inadequate or feels like giving up.

Symbols and signs help a child to understand the process of communication though, which is essential for productive speech. They start to understand what it's all about. Handing over a symbol is exactly the same as using speech, it's just a different medium.

Unfortunately, if a child has no adequate alternative to speech, then you are left with yet another layer of parenting, caused by frustration. So, while you're waiting for the bus, it's a good idea to explore other options.

The bus may or may not arrive, but this won't hurt and in fact it will benefit them, I promise. I know this because of my experience with Bobby.

Bobby's speech started after he had learnt Makaton sign language and the first words he said were those he had learnt to sign. I don't think this is a coincidence.

Tori first suggested the Picture Exchange Communication System (PECS) before Alec started primary school. She noticed that he could recognise a packet of chocolate buttons very easily and thought that it would be good to try. Since we tried symbols early, he was using symbols that were meaningful to him (biscuit, cake) by the time he started school.

After he became used to symbols, Alec started to make intentional sounds, too. When he says 'VAH-VAH!' it means he extra-especially wants something. He has developed it for comic effect, too, with 'VAH-VAH VAH VAH VAH VAH!' meaning 'Do it and do it now!' Lately, his voice has broken, so we get a mixture of treble and bass VAH-VAHs.

Now that he can communicate non-verbally and with some intentional sounds, my main focus is on reducing the anxiety caused by Alec's autism by using photographs and symbols.

It all takes preparation, time and, above all, thought – which is the most precious parenting resource of all.

Alec had his first trip to the orthodontist this morning to see whether it was worth putting him under a general anaesthetic to sort out a rogue canine.

The short answer was 'No.'

There are no shortcuts, however, when it comes to preparing Alec for a trip to a new surgery.

Alongside my work to-do list, I keep a personal to-do list. If we're going anywhere, this to-do list includes 'picture story for Alec'. Before I start any work for the day, I check I'm up to date with his picture stories.

Yesterday, I sat down and thought about what Alec really needed to know. This makes you genuinely expert at cutting to the chase when it comes to verbal language, by the way. Since having Alec, I waffle less. Well, most of the time.

First, he needed to know what the new surgery looked like. In this respect, Google Images is my saviour. He needed to know what the new orthodontist looked like – I Googled her image, too. Last, I Googled a cartoon image of a dentist with a boy in the big dentist chair. The 'big chair' is a really good visual to orientate Alec because you only find those at dentists, so it's great shorthand.

Also, Alec likes the Big Chair because it usually comes with an automatic up and down button, which is a bit like being on a slow fairground ride. Alec likes anything that moves at the touch of a button. One holiday cottage we hired a few years back happened to come with a stair lift and as we passed the hallway we'd regularly wave to Alec as he spent the entire evening slowly moving up and downstairs with a self-satisfied grin on his face.

After the dentist images, I typed 'THEN' and added his school logo (easily recognisable to Alec) and a picture of his teacher. So, if you think you're going home afterwards, matey, think again.

Then I got Alec's 'change' symbol out and went upstairs, where he was doing his best to avoid bedtime.

'Alec, I have something to show you,' I said. He looked up from his iPad and looked at the A4 paper in my hand, not exactly interested but half-heartedly noting it. He knows immediately that this means change. As with most parenting in the autism world, if you do it enough times, experience can fill in the gaps that nature didn't automatically complete.

I signed 'tomorrow' and slowly went through the pictures and explained about the appointment. I did it twice. My main worry is that if Alec talks, the first thing he will say is, 'Why have you been telling me everything twice for the last ten years?'

Sometimes, it's hard to know whether something has gone in. I ask, 'Do you understand?' and he signs 'Yes', but 'Yes' is his general method of shutting me up. I remember from my own experience, there is nothing more annoying than your mother telling you something repeatedly when you are a teenager. So, I left it and hoped for the best.

This morning, as we are getting dressed, I show him the pictures again and the 'change' card. As we're in the car, I explain that we're going straight on this time, not left.

You may think this is a lengthy process. If you want a lengthier process, then don't do any preparation at all. Then enjoy a happy half hour fending Alec off in the car, trying to keep both hands on the steering wheel and not really getting there at all.

Alec used to be extremely passive and never needed any explanations. He's 13 now and not at all passive. In some ways, this is a good sign – it shows he's more aware of his surroundings and his feelings. In other ways, it's basically not good, especially as he thinks he's a better driver than me, although, to be fair, he has often reminded me correctly when I should be in third gear.

Once we're there, Alec gives a few loud whoops in the waiting room. These days, I don't care at all. They knew they had an autistic kid coming. If they keep him waiting, they can expect a bit of noise. Might hurry them up a bit. It's a private orthodontist but this just refers to the price and not the speed of service as far as I can tell.

During our appointment, the orthodontist asks Alec to bite his teeth together. Alec can't understand this, as he has learnt that all dentists expect you to say, 'Ahhh!' He dutifully opens his mouth wide several times. When he does finally clamp it shut, it's over her mirror.

Afterwards, once persuaded that the mirror wasn't a take-home souvenir, he was delivered safely back to school without incident and got a fruity yo-yo chew as a reward for being so flexible. My handbag has emergency fruity yo-yo rations for every situation. This is because fruity yo-yos can be twiddled as well as eaten so can be extremely handy.

A lot of stuff written on communicating with non-verbal children can put parents off. It's made out to be quite complicated and they fear getting something wrong.

Forget all that – you can't go 'wrong' when you're talking to your own child as long as you're aware of their needs.

What I love about working with Tori, now my *AuKids* magazine co-editor, is that she understands how it works in the real world. Use a piece of paper and pen, a photo from your phone, anything to hand, she always says. Language is an immediate thing – you can't always prepare beautiful pictures or wait for the laminator to warm up. Use what you know your child will understand.

> **Forget all that – you can't go 'wrong' when you're talking to your own child as long as you're aware of their needs.**

Having symbols to hand that you know they will regularly use, or having what we call a visual timetable – symbols for tasks done in a regular routine, like getting dressed – can really help even if they understand the spoken word. The symbol makes it more solid and easier to process. I always start from Alec's point of view. His picture books are made up of things that he might want to say to me.

One of the most tiresome things is keeping a symbol book up to date. If you're going to use it, then when they grow out of interests (say from Postman Pat to Toy Story) you have to update your image library. Alec has matured now to the point where he enjoys music videos. He needs the language to tell me whether he wants me to download a guitar song or a piano one.

If I ever sigh to myself and think that this is laborious and a pain in the neck, I just have to think of what I'd do in Alec's position if I had no way of saying that I wanted to watch *Coronation Street*, or wanted a coffee not a tea, or preferred a bath to a shower. A second or two of thinking that is enough to persuade me that this is worth my trouble.

My main method of communication with Alec isn't something that I was taught. I use my two fists to ask him to select a preference. It's just the quickest, easiest way of making a choice. Tea or coffee? I ask him. Salt 'n' vinegar or cheese and onion? Marmite or jam? He gets to choose. If I ask Bobby his opinion, I ask Alec too, just in a different way.

. . . .

Without being asked your opinion, you don't learn to form one.

. . . .

He gets to choose. That's so important.

Until he was asked for his opinions, I don't think that Alec knew he had any. Without being asked for your opinion, you don't learn to form one.

So, you don't develop a solid sense of who you are. We're all made up of opinions. Being asked for your view, however small the decision, and having your choices valued is key to developing a sense of self.

It's not just about preventing frustration, it's so much more than that.

Tori and I sat down one day and thought about all the tiny choices I made for Alec that he could make for himself. There were tons of them. Now I ask him which top he wants to wear, even though I know he's not that bothered. Or I ask him which cereal he would like. Most of the time he chooses Weetabix but occasionally he fancies a change and asks for Shreddies. And the thing is, he has the power to change his mind if he wants to.

You can't speak for them. They have to use their own voice, even if it's without words. Only then will they grow into truly independent spirits.

John Lennon once said that life is what happens to you while you are busy making other plans.

Communication is what happens while you're waiting for your child to speak.

9 It's Not Your Place or Mine... It's a Bit of Both

Entering the autistic world

Debby: 'Bobby, if you help me find my pink USB stick, then I'll give you a big present.'

Bobby: 'OKAY!'

(Two-minute pause.)

Bobby: 'Mum, if you help me find your USB stick I'll give you all my very own love.'

People who haven't met Bobby before tell me that he's really self-assured. Other children seem drawn to him because he has absolutely no argument with his own autism. He accepts himself – and I think most of the time he likes himself. So, he seems quite a confident child, unfussed about what others may think of him.

Ironically, since he doesn't care much about whether other people like him or not, they tend to like him.

I remember during his first week at secondary school, I asked Bobby if he had found anyone he wanted to be friends with yet.

'Not yet, Mum, I'm just concentrating on surviving it right now,' he said.

What he meant was – adapting to change took a lot of energy and there would be time to make friends later. No rush. He had started to realise what worked for him. This came from a confident inner core.

Without language, Alec seems to create much the same impression. I am often told that he 'seems very happy in his own skin'.

Is this nature or nurture?

It's probably a bit of both, but I like to think that some of it is because of their parents' attitude to their differences and how we have conveyed that to them over the years.

In terms of 'your place or mine?', we've accepted that we'll share a bit of both, and this has had a profound effect on both twins.

If you want your autistic child to join the non-autistic world, to behave like a non-autistic person and to 'fit in', then please accept that they may get close but, however hard they try, they may never be able to duplicate something that doesn't come naturally to them.

Ultimately, this may disappoint you, but worst of all it will disappoint *them*.

They may not be able to understand why they're trying to act like others when they don't share the same thought patterns. It really is just pretending.

It's important to remember that a child's view of the world begins and ends with their parents. Your expectations become theirs. If you are disappointed in them, they will be even more downcast about themselves.

Even if you don't say it, they can tell.

I guess you may well be tired of me making this point, but it really isn't necessary for them to fit in *that much* in order for you to be happy as a family or for them to be successful as individuals.

When it comes to an autistic child letting you in, if you really want that to happen, you have to start by giving off the vibe that their perspective of the world is valid.

When it comes to 'your place or mine?', then let's not think of the autistic mind as the holiday cottage from hell. It has to be somewhere we're prepared to visit, to sit down in, to stay for a while (even if we aren't always offered a cup of tea the minute we step through the door).

When it comes to an autistic child letting you in, if you really want that to happen, you have to start by giving off the vibe that their perspective of the world is valid.

Only then can you truly start to share experiences with your child. If you complain to yourself, 'They're never in my world,' ask yourself if you're ever prepared to visit theirs.

Olga Bogdashina often uses her talks to point out that we 'blame' autistic people for not being able to guess what's in non-autistic minds (or for lacking 'Theory of Mind') when we are truly dreadful at understanding what's in theirs.

I liked that point. So I nicked it.

Sometimes, in my haste to help Bobby qualify as a Top Bloke Liked By All, I've forgotten that what's important to him isn't the same as what's important to me.

He reminded me of this when I showed him a 'cool' new top I'd bought for him. 'No. I don't wanna wear it,' he said.

'But why, Bobby? It's really cool.'

'Mum, you don't have to *look* cool to *be* cool.'

Why was it so important for me that my son was made to look 'on trend', when it didn't really reflect who he was at all? He was simply being honest.

I've learnt a lot of lessons from him.

When Bobby was younger, I joined the social circus alongside all the other parents. If Bobby received 30 miniature Christmas cards from children he didn't know well, I would write 30 mini Christmas cards back. I'd choose them carefully – too cheap and it would look like we didn't care (we didn't); too glitzy and it would look as if we were trying too hard, and it doesn't do for the autistic kid to appear desperate for friendship.

Bobby was about eight at the time.

I had better things to think about, like whether our tree's baubles would survive Alec's constant heavy-handed curiosity, but I was focusing on this instead.

Er, excuse me…

Why would writing 30 Christmas cards on Bobby's behalf help my son to fit in? I was just joining in the whole fake social pantomime, one that he refused to take part in, and for good reason. Bobby didn't even look at the cards he received. I'd find half a dozen hugging the bottom of his schoolbag in January.

He knew that most of them were meaningless.

Teaching your kids social rules relies on the same kind of attitude as the rest of autism parenting. Pick your battles. Do they need to learn how to sit quietly in assembly? Yes, it's a valuable lesson for life. Do they need to be able to write crappy little Christmas cards to people they don't know or like much? No, they don't.

Is it parental anxiety that causes us to try so hard, or is it truly helpful to our children? I had to ask myself that question quite a lot. My idea of being sociable is different to Bobby's. He has less of a need for it and is satisfied (being a bloke) with less emotional depth to his friendships too.

Sometimes, autistic people have a damn good point. They expose our little social niceties for the truly meaningless rituals they really are.

Once I knew more about autism, had got beyond the 'Triad of Impairments' and had started to see that elements of it were well worth valuing, I learnt not to be plagued by the need to reprogramme my kids.

Accepted for who they were, their self-esteem started to blossom. Ironically, this led to them relaxing and behaving in a more laid-back way. Let's face it, most of the problems we encounter as parents are not to do with the autism itself but the distressed behaviour connected with it.

You can immediately reduce that pressure by accepting who they are.

One of my earliest lessons in life was from a Danny Kaye cassette I owned aged ten. In the musical story 'Tubby the Tuba', Tubby hated his own tuba sound and wanted to sound like a 'better' instrument.

Eventually, Tubby learnt that his band actually sounded rubbish without his 'oom pah-pahs'.

It took some other members of the band to point this out to him, though.

Forgive me if this isn't the best synopsis that you've ever read but it was a long time ago.

The thing is, there are plenty of socially adaptable, interpersonally gifted people in the world. We need people who think a little differently – we need people who are more prepared to focus on things rather than get distracted by other people, their assumptions and their reactions. We need people who are concrete thinkers with attention to detail.

Yet with autism, our children are constantly learning that being themselves isn't quite good enough.

Autistic boys tend to get a bit down about this, but the effect on autistic girls is even more worrying. They become expert at mirroring others' behaviour and sometimes they fool everyone. It takes a huge toll on them, to the point that they become uncertain of who they really are. Fortunately, we're starting to wake up to the difficulties that girls face and many superb authors, including Jennifer Cook O'Toole, my personal favourite, are spreading awareness.

I was always conscious that learning he was different would have an adverse effect on Bobby. So right from the word go, we emphasised the stuff he was brilliant at and praised his successes.

Bobby's failures were always huge in his own head. He assumed that you had to be able to do something perfectly first time, or you were a total failure.

It was easy to see why. Early maths came to him so easily and so did computers. Whenever he had to try for something that he didn't automatically pick up, it was a painful contrast. He had to learn that failure is part of learning (for some great advice on this, read *Self-Regulation in Everyday Life: A How-To Guide for Parents* (MacKenzie and Preveza 2015)).

You can't hide from an autistic child that they struggle with certain things – that's reality. I wanted Bobby to know that this struggle wasn't his own fault but was due to having autism. So, when he was very young, I explained autism extremely simply.

'There are some things your brain is very fast at and there are some things that it finds difficult,' I said. 'That's because you have something called autism. Your brain works a bit differently to other people's.'

Not wrong, not brilliant, just different. Neutral.

What he lacked in certain areas, he made up for in others.

The trouble with having a 'diagnosis' and using words like 'therapy' is that it creates an assumption that in terms of 'your place or mine?', our non-autistic place is always the preferable one. By adopting this as a goal, you're constantly pulling your child away from their natural state. That tug of war is very wearing. Sometimes it's necessary but sometimes it really isn't.

Once I realised that Bobby was learning, healthy and perfectly happy, I thought that working to change him might be a bit of a pointless exercise. I could give him strategies to work on the things that caused him upset, stress or isolated him. The rest I'd leave well alone.

> **Autism is really very simple to understand if you think of the autism brain as a museum that is only open to the public by prior arrangement.**

You could argue, 'Well you have to change them, otherwise they'll never survive in the "real world".' That's very true. They do need to learn how to visit Non-Autistic Land and how to survive in it. Social skills need to be taught to equip them for the pervading culture. They need to become aware of their behaviour and how that impacts on everyone else.

In short, they need extra lessons in life and that's a darn hard challenge for them.

In Bobby's case, I always made it clear, however, that behaviour was separate from personality. There were things he could learn to make life easier, but I wasn't going to change who he was.

Learning our non-autistic rules makes Bobby an autistic person who has learnt social skills, not a 'neurotypical' person. So I'm never surprised if, after all that hard work, he wants to retreat into his world.

That place may feel a bit alien to you, but no less alien than your world is to your autistic child.

Autism is really very simple to understand if you think of the autism brain as a museum that is only open to the public by prior arrangement.

Everything in your child's brain is neatly ordered just the way they like it and, what's more, not all thoughts are for sharing, they are just for examining within. The last thing they want is a load of unpredictable visitors coming in and smashing the place up.

Alec sometimes wants to walk around his own museum without interruption. I have often been torn as to whether I interrupt his repetitious behaviour or leave him to it. Sometimes I can see that his repetition is through boredom and habit and I distract him.

However, if he's been busy and had a lot of demands placed on him (like after school) I expect him to retreat to his own museum for a bit.

I don't fully understand it, but I respect it.

My best chance of bonding with Bobby is visiting his world (his museum) when I'm invited. He tells me about his specialisms. I listen and I ask questions. He learns how to have a conversation by talking about something that feels like home to him.

In this way, by me visiting his comfort zone, he is more adaptable when he gets outside it.

I see friends and family trying hard to communicate with Bobby by asking him questions based on what they feel may be of interest to him. 'How is school?' for instance. They may not get that far. Things move along a lot faster when they lean over Bobby as he plays a game on his iPad and say, 'Tell me about this game, what do you have to do?' They are popping into his world. It's that easy!

We can visit our children's museums when we know their interests, but what about non-verbal children? How do we visit their world?

In Alec's case, it's easy to show him he is accepted for who he is. I just watch him play; I sometimes play the same thing next to him without making demands and join in with what he asks me to. He doesn't ask me verbally. He asks me with his body language, with his smiles and with his hands.

When he fills my hands with marbles, I ask him what I should do next. He shows me by reaching his hands up in the air. He wants me to drop them from a height. I obey and then he carefully fills my hands again. It took many years for Alec to trust that I was a worthy playmate. Years of watching and waiting and joining in only when invited to.

After diagnosis, I had a misleading understanding of the word 'therapy'. Therapy meant hard work.

To bring my twins' development forward, I should be doing hard work and so should they. This is the British way. Work hard for rewards. Nothing is gained by doing nothing.

Except, with autism it's quite different.

Gradually I learnt, through Tori's teaching and through my own experience, that my kids became sponges when they were having a laugh. On the other hand, when Alec thought I was in 'education' mode, his brain would become a brick – he would sense it and switch off.

We used to have a lot of fun hiding under duvets in the dark, saying 'dark!' and 'spooky!' and finding light-up things to play with.

One game that Alec particularly liked was to be rolled up in a duvet. No doubt this gave him some sensory pressure that he enjoyed. As I rolled, I'd say, 'Caterpillar, caterpillar, caterpillar…' When he was rolled up tight I'd say, 'Cocoon!' and when he escaped, I'd say, 'BUTTERFLY!'

He thought this hilarious and tried to say 'Butterfly'. It was just a laugh, but we both got a lot out of it. Natural interaction has always been his best source of learning.

Alec's dad hasn't done much formal autism reading. What he's learnt, he's learnt through me. Yet during Dad's Tickle Time, Alec speaks more than he does at any other time of the day. He is so excited by the tickles that he will attempt a countdown from ten. He requests with his own language. And now when I sign, 'Would you like Dad to come upstairs?' he nods his fist vigorously – the yes sign – and vocalises with his VAH-VAH-VAH-VAH!

Alec's learning is just incorporated into his daily routines, focusing on what he wants and what he likes. Making the most of the 'aut' part of 'autism'.

In the early years, when I was working with Tori for Alec's speech and language therapy, she taught me a lesson that's stayed with me ever since.

'When you join in with what they're doing, what do you think you're showing them?' she asked me. I gave a few weedy suggestions. 'Yes, and you're also showing them that their idea is good, it's okay, it's okay to be doing what they're doing. It's not wrong. It reinforces them and that gives them confidence to build on their communication.'

Oooh. I'd never thought of it like that.

Joining in with them not only gives them the opportunity to communicate with you. It gives them confidence, too.

Some time later, I was at a social gathering and I was watching a parent of a child who didn't have autism playing with her little girl. They were looking at a game and the mother was constantly 'correcting' the child. 'No look, you do it like this!'

Given my autism training, my firsts clenched slightly and it was all I could do not to start preaching. I was starting to see how autism parenting could benefit everyone.

Their museum is a world where an autistic child can retreat to, and you're very privileged if you're invited. But you won't always be welcome and that's important to remember.

Alec right this minute is less interested in me than he is in replaying a small section of the old-style Paddington Bear in which our furry hero makes his own toffee and gets tummy ache. Paddington's 'Woegrrhhggh' sound seems to appeal to the extent that Alec has worked out the slow-motion button on the remote control.

There's no point in trying to understand this.

A bit of your world, a bit of our world, there's a healthy balance to be had.

The museum gates do open for some sociable time, on the specific terms of the management.

When Alec and Bobby open those museum doors and let you in, it's pretty special. You've earned it. That's how autism works. People with autism don't lie and pretend that they like you, nor can they force themselves to be sociable when they really don't feel like it.

Alone time is important recharging time for Alec and Bobby. I test the social waters by keeping them company. If Alec snuggles up to me while he's watching Paddington, he's fine with me visiting the Alec Museum. When we are playing with fidget spinners together, and I'm about as mesmerised as him, it's no longer a case of 'your place or mine?', it's a bit of both.

I'm perfectly prepared for my kids to be in their own worlds sometimes if it makes them happy, so long as they can meet me in mine often enough that we can communicate with each other.

It's not 'your place or mine?', it's somewhere in between. You may not triumph if you insist on 'my place', since autistic kids need to retreat to their own worlds in order to cope with ours.

Home is the place where the pressure eases off, so be wary of therapies that put your kids under extra stress in the place where they should feel the least pressure to 'perform'.

Autistic traits have a purpose and that purpose is often survival and defence.

Over the last ten years, I've learnt to respect that, even if I don't always understand it.

Sometimes, without being autistic yourself, this is just the best a parent can do.

Of course, parents can't take all the credit for confident youngsters. Other people have something to do with that too. Which leads me nicely on to the next chapter...

It's like I planned this or something.

10 Hell Is Other People

Tackling problems at school

Age ten, Bobby about to sneeze: 'Ah-Ah-Ah... Oh. Cancelled.'

Have you ever owned an orchid? They have a reputation for being difficult to grow. In fact, they aren't that fussy, they just need a particular set of circumstances in which to thrive. Those conditions are different from other house plants, but once they get them they do very well. They grow into beautiful, exotic plants and are reasonably easy to manage.

Autistic children are just like orchids. All they need is the right environment. That's why Tori and I called our magazine *AuKids*. I can't take the credit for the orchid story, that was Tori's idea. My friend is beautifully in touch with horticulture. NOT. If you want a plant to die, just hand it to Tori. She knows a good analogy when she sees one, though.

In his novel, *Huis Clos*, Jean-Paul Sartre said that hell is other people (Gore and Sartre 1987). Most of the problems our kids experience aren't really caused by their autism at all. They're caused by the environment. Unsurprisingly, a major element of our environment is other people. And yet we overlook that quite a lot.

We spend a lot of time and energy avoiding overloading environments, but perhaps we should be focusing just as much on helping others to understand our kids.

We spend a lot of time and energy avoiding overloading environments, but perhaps we should be focusing just as much on helping others to understand our kids.

It only takes one glance at Autcraft, the first Minecraft server for children with autism, to witness the difference that a positive environment can make.

When you read Autcraft dialogue, you can't tell that its players have autism. They certainly don't seem to show any social difficulties. In fact, they're politer to each other than on most other gaming forums.

Why? They're in their home environment, playing a game they like with people who understand them. In addition, they are focused on a joint venture rather than purely socialising, which brings out the best in them. Finally, there is no pressure to be present and no one is judging their body language. They can play as disembodied souls, free to be themselves.

This is why it's so important to get the right environment for our kids. When they've got it, they truly become themselves.

Most of the letters we receive about lack of understanding in education are, unsurprisingly, not about special schools but about mainstream provision.

Let's skip the chapter on woefully inadequate autism training for schools and cut to the chase. Given what we know to be widespread misunderstanding of autism and budgetary restrictions on resources, how do you ensure a positive schooling experience for your child?

I've had unusually good experiences with both my boys' primary and secondary schools – a special one in Alec's case and mainstream in Bobby's. Some of this was down to pure good fortune, some of it was down to planning and some of it was down to working with them.

None of it was down to biffing a teacher over the head with a frying pan, so I wouldn't recommend this even on the occasions when you are tempted.

There are some things in life you can't affect. I'm aiming to help with the bits that you can. If someone is going to sign their child up for a school that doesn't get autism, don't let it be you.

My first tip is to obey your instinct. This is what I did and it served me well. I have known parents who have overridden an uneasy feeling right from the start because the school was a practical choice.

Instinct isn't daft. It's a thousand tiny decisions formed through impressions

> **Instinct isn't daft. It's a thousand tiny decisions formed through impressions made in a split second. It leaves you with a feeling, and you should trust it.**

made in a split second. It leaves you with a feeling, and you should trust it.

Funnily enough, people seem to trust their instinct when it comes to choosing houses more than when it comes to choosing schools. I've no idea why. Can you picture your son or daughter there? Can you imagine them happy?

Second tip, don't just look at the pretty collages on the walls and decide that the place looks clean. Listen closely to what's being said to you.

One of the best-kept primary schools that I looked around was, in my opinion, the worst choice for autism. Its website looked lovely, it had a posh reputation and its Ofsted results were great.

When I came to look around, though, no one greeted me for some time and eventually the SENCO (special educational needs co-ordinator) arrived and talked about the school as we walked down corridors, never once considering that I'd like a sit-down chat. What she knew about autism you could write on the back of a postage stamp. Not a large one. I wasn't really looking at the neat pens and the tidy rows of books. I was listening to the warning siren in my soul that said, 'Get out fast!'

In contrast, the school I actually chose was a little scruffier in comparison. The headteacher greeted me enthusiastically and sat me down. 'Now. Tell me about Bobby!' he said, and from that moment I was sold. He knew what it was about. It was about checking that their provision could match my son's needs. Does the school ask questions and show real interest in your child?

Bear in mind that a school's culture comes from the top, so it's really important to know that the headteacher understands and is behind a truly inclusive environment.

My third tip is to watch how other autistic children are getting on in the classroom if you can. At the 'perfect' primary school that I looked around, the SENCO proudly showed me her version of inclusion. The class were at one end of the room and a lad with autism was at the other, working completely separately with a teaching assistant. Being in the same room isn't inclusion. It's being in the same room.

When I was shown around Bobby's secondary school, several things caught my eye. In the first secondary school that I'd looked around, I'd shown the special needs team a picture of Bobby and his recent report. He wasn't there and I wanted them to be able to visualise the subject of our discussions. They virtually threw them over their shoulders in a stunning display of indifference.

Then in solemn tones (despite my smiles) they talked about him needing to 'fit in' and the limitations on any adaptations they could make, as if it was both as expensive and as complicated as rocket science. My son was to be a distraction from the pupils who could really do well. He was an inconvenience. They didn't say it; they might as well have, though.

I left raging and disgusted. Don't worry, I wrote them a long letter and copied in the council's head of special needs (and they were completely, predictably defensive about it).

In short, I'm going to be really arrogant here: I don't care if all your friends are raving about a particular school.

I don't even care if all the kids are going there and you are worried about your child being separated from their friends. A bad environment simply isn't worth it.

Bobby, by the way, was separated from his best friend. He got another one and he stayed in touch with his old one. So now he has two.

The other thing to consider, especially as they get older, is how autism is explained to their peer group. A good school will make provision for this and have a culture of understanding.

There were several factors that made me want to head through the foyer of Bobby's new secondary school on roller skates shouting, 'YES PLEASE! SIGN US UP NOW!' It was not only the provision that I was told about, but also the subtler signs around the school. The tortoises for the special needs kids to look after; the special open morning for the supported children; the inspiring notices with inclusive messages aimed at all pupils dotted around the school; and the many quiet places he could escape to, both indoors and outside.

And finally, the *pièce de résistance*, the reaction to him from other pupils. Bobby came with us to the open evening when there were a lot of existing pupils around. The school is split into five colleges, each associated with a different colour, and he had already learnt that pupils' tie colour indicated their college.

He approached two boys, pointed at their ties and guessed their colleges. Then he flapped excitedly.

I waited for their sidelong glances at each other. My parental radar is finely tuned when it comes to other children being cruel. There were no glances. They just smiled and explained. After we walked away, I looked back at them. They weren't nudging each other and giggling. These kids were used to being around children who were different.

Once you've chosen a school, that's where the real fun begins. It starts and ends with the way that you communicate.

A parent's ability to influence other people with their positive attitude is perhaps the most underestimated of all the special powers we have.

If you have the ability to influence people's thinking, you can change how they feel. Change how they feel and you've changed how they cope.

When I introduce Bobby and Alec – whether I'm talking about them at a conference or I'm describing them to a new support worker – I always start with what's brilliant about them. 'You'll love Bobby!' I say. 'He's hilarious!', or, 'Alec is the sweetest, most laid-back dude I know.'

I try to do this even if I'm having an off day, one of those I'd Rather Not Be A Parent days. But why do I do it?

Call it a keen interest in psychology and imagine this scenario…

You're at a cocktail party. I know, given your lifestyle you go to loads of them, right? Well, you are, you're here at my imaginary cocktail party. Make the most.

I haven't met you before, and someone brings you over to me. 'I don't believe you've met,' she starts and then proceeds to tell me all about your worst personality traits. OMG, you have so many…

My smile starts to fade and I make some excuse about needing to find another drink. You're the last person I'm going to hang out with tonight.

This is what some parents do when handing over their child for the first time to someone new. I understand it. The thought behind it is, 'Will you cope with the worst my child can throw at you?' You don't want them to get a nasty surprise by pretending everything is perfect, do you?

I'm not suggesting you hide for one second that your son likes to remove wallpaper when a room isn't quite ready for redecorating or that your daughter when challenged has a Top C that would shatter a window five miles away.

The best results, however, come when someone WANTS to do a job. To start by knowing the most rewarding aspects of a task makes us more enthusiastic about it. If we champion our kids and show everyone what we love about them, other carers form their initial impressions based on the upside and are far more likely to respond better to the challenges.

· ·

If we champion our kids and show everyone what we love about them, other carers form their initial impressions based on the upside and are far more likely to respond better to the challenges.

· ·

When I was studying English Literature, I used to find myself in the psychology section of the library, which

I found a bit more interesting. I read one study that said the impression we form of someone – positive or negative – is then reinforced by everything they subsequently do. We see it through that positive or negative 'filter'.

You know it yourself, when you think about it. If someone you like does something thoughtless, you say to yourself they were busy. If someone you don't like does something thoughtless, they are confirmed as the dastardliest dregs of the dustbin.

By championing your child, you turn those around them into positive thinkers.

I am afraid I've no idea which psychology study I read, as I should have been writing something on *Tamburlaine the Great* at the time, but if you are familiar with it, let me know.

The second major factor in giving your child a promising start is to furnish their teachers with the full picture.

Call me pessimistic, but I have always assumed that unless people have tons of quality information about Bobby and Alec, they will make mistakes.

Arm them. Arm them to the teeth like they are the best kitted out squadron on the battlefield.

Honestly, this is where a stitch in time saves nine. Effort made building up a full picture before a new introduction saves an awful lot of bother further down the line.

You can use a 'portfolio', which is just a little guide you've written on your child.

Or, I have a chart that I use for Bobby, with classroom tips on it. It lists the difficulties he faces and what works best in response. The tips chart has been built up over the years with his teaching assistant and myself adding to it, and has been passed on to the secondary school.

Home–school diaries are brilliant, too.

I've been known to drop an email in to school at 8am, too (I did it this morning), warning that a late night had led to a less-than-enthusiastic response in the morning. In the rush, Bobby started getting very agitated. As he left for school, I figured that even though a meltdown wasn't imminent, it would only take one little extra push to cause one. So, I told the teachers. It's what we call a 'foot off the pedal day'. A stitch in time…

Following the championing mentality, keep your teachers' energy levels high by focusing on positive achievements and acknowledging the effort that they're making on your child's behalf.

So instead of using the diary just to note problems, use it to say, 'Thank you!' or 'That's great!' or 'I really enjoyed reading that!' Yes, it's a job to them, but they're only human. Everyone gets encouraged by a little praise. Don't assume that they get it enough. They never do.

I like to reinforce good practice by emailing little thank yous when something has gone particularly well, occasionally writing to the headteacher to let them know how appreciative I am of their staff's efforts.

Mostly, I just want them to be acknowledged. Also, just as there's nothing in the word 'no' that tells a child what they should be doing, having discussions only when there are problems doesn't really reinforce the good stuff. It doesn't take a minute.

Most parents only talk to school when there is a problem. If you communicate through the good times as well as the bad, they'll be able say to themselves when things DO go wrong, 'This parent is not usually a complainer.' You will look more balanced.

Even at the best schools you hit the odd hitch and the key to knowing whether you can remain working with them is how they respond to these.

This is why I feel it's so important to leave the boxing gloves at home. You can't properly tell what a school's intentions are when staff are on the defensive.

If, having had reasonable and productive discussions on a number of occasions, you have witnessed no positive change whatsoever, I give you permission to reach for the boxing gloves.

When you get emotional, unfortunately it starts to sound as if your feelings have got in the way of good judgement. They may not have done, but that's how it comes across.

I've found a good technique to stop me from getting too emotional is to describe a situation pairing cause with effect, rather than focusing on how I feel about it (which is like killing someone).

For example: 'There was a fire alarm this morning. Because Bobby wasn't warned about it, he wasn't expecting it. His autism means that unexpected changes are extremely stressful for him. This is why he panicked. What can we do in future?'

Obviously, the answer is to warn him about the damn fire alarm, but if you draw the answer from someone else and it looks like their idea, it makes them feel more in control. This means they're far more likely to change their practice than if you stormed in the office shouting, 'Warn him about the fire alarm next time, you NITWITS!'

I mean, that may help, but it doesn't really create a great working relationship and it doesn't lead to better understanding.

Inviting opinions even if you don't agree with them makes people feel listened to and is more likely to make them listen to you in return. Phrases that aren't accusing and nudge them towards joint working work really well, such as, 'What can we do?' and 'I'd like to know your thoughts.'

Finally, don't jump to conclusions. I did once and I'm so glad I didn't act on it. It appeared as if Bobby's timetable had been changed overnight. My initial reaction was, 'WHAT THE HECK IS GOING ON HERE?' I wrote a polite email that started, 'Any reason why...?'

The answer was that he'd got the wrong timetable by mistake. I could have wrecked a good relationship with an assumption. It's very hard not to make assumptions when things haven't been great in the past, but I do try to judge each situation separately. This is easy for me because there's a basic trust. If the school hasn't earned your trust, it's much harder.

In autism, a child's communication skills are compromised. That means parents have to be doubly good at communicating on their behalf. If we aren't, meltdowns surely follow.

It's a bit more bother, but it's worth it.

End note

I haven't got lots more room to go into what happens if
school really doesn't listen to you, but happily in the UK we
now have the law on our side under the Equality Act 2010.
The website www.inclusivechoice.com offers some great
information and training on it and, if you're in the UK,
I'd also recommend IPSEA (Independent Parental Special
Education Advice): www.ipsea.org.uk.

11 You Can Learn What You Lack

Getting to know other people's thoughts

Bobby, age 11: 'Not even God could wrap my blankie. I have been given the mystic power.'

One of my early lessons in autism was understanding that my twins thought I was a mind-reader.

Later this news was broken to me in a more scholarly way, dressed up as the Theory of Mind. Apparently, Bobby and Alec lacked it.

Theory of Mind is not as technical as it sounds. It's that loathsome jargon again.

Simply put, your child's mind cannot jump positions from one perspective to another. That's where the 'aut' from 'autism' comes from. Autistic people take a single perspective – their own.

So, the reason they weren't asking me for things is because I already knew what they wanted, didn't I? Weren't we sharing the same thought?

I taught them I couldn't read their minds by refusing to guess what they wanted, even though it was quite obvious to me. It took patience and a certain amount of nerve. Pretending to be stupid was something that came naturally, though.

If they started to try to tell me what they wanted, I was taught to 'model' what it was they would say if they could. Tori taught me to do this. 'I'd like milk please!'

The idea that your inner experience is not the same as someone else's is an extremely tough one to get across to an autistic child.

Switching perspectives comes so naturally to me that it's very difficult to imagine life without it. As I'm writing this book, I'm thinking 'from me, to you, from me, to you...' constantly trying to predict how you are receiving the information I write.

I have to address multiple perspectives. You might be reading this already knowing plenty about autism but just wanting some light relief or, having mastered the theory, to colour in the blanks where 'lived experience' should be. Or, you might know very little about autism and this is your first dip into the subject.

Then again, you might be a reader of *AuKids* magazine and anxious for a behind-the-scenes glimpse. Or your experiences in some ways may be truly similar to my own and you might well be able to nod and laugh with me, which gives us both a kick. I do hope so.

This book has to be ready for all those perspectives and believe me it isn't easy. I may occasionally fail to address the needs you have, and sorry about that.

Let's just say that it's good enough that I know those different perspectives are out there.

To someone who can't grasp this idea, it must seem as if the world constantly DOESN'T GET IT. I firmly believe that developing Theory of Mind, the ability to switch perspectives and guess motivations, is key to developing both social and communication skills.

Having a perspective on what others think and what influences them leads to good interpersonal skills. The better your skill, the more likely your ability to convince people that your ideas are better than theirs – hence leaders are born.

So, despite its very dull appearance, the concept of Theory of Mind is something we as parents should probably get to grips with.

Some children with autism don't talk because they don't feel the need to get their message across. It's not that they can't (unless they have a physical reason), or won't, it's that they don't see the point.

Autistic speaker Ros Blackburn (2011) said that she only started talking when she was frustrated enough with people to do so. Up until her teens, she had managed to get what she wanted without having to bother.

If you lack Theory of Mind, it follows that you don't feel judged and that you don't judge others.

Think about that for a mo. I know I am. I think I might even have to get a coffee at this point.

In the same talk, I remember Ros saying that autistic people don't tend to get embarrassed because they honestly can't imagine what other people think of them. This is a superb way to be if you are talking to huge crowds at conferences.

When I get up to speak at conferences, I am plagued by what others may be thinking. It's a gruesome feeling that most of us are probably only too familiar with.

It's not that autistic people are deeply arrogant. It's just very hard for them to imagine their audience's perspective. So, predicting how someone receives the information and tailoring it to suit them isn't in their repertoire.

I spoke to my friend Tim (*AuKids'* autism advocate) about this. I asked him whether he ever thought about what other people might be listening for or what they may be thinking during a conversation.

He said he didn't and he couldn't; he found it impossible. As a child, he was used to bad reactions to him and to save time he just assumed that every kind of negative mood must be something to do with him. He didn't know why.

You'll probably hear this phrase from autistic people quite a lot: 'Must be something I've done.' Bobby uses the phrase, 'Sorry about that,' which he uses as an umbrella term to cover his uncertainty. He uses it often, it's a just-in-case phrase.

Rubbish isn't it, to feel as if you're failing but not to be able to pinpoint what it is you're doing wrong?

As a parent, I see it as my job to be honest with Bobby. I point out cause and effect of all behaviours – not just his – all the time.

Once again, the Lego® building analogy comes in handy. We have a normal conversation, but I give many more explanations than I would to someone else.

So, I tell him that if he doesn't reply when I call him for dinner, I think he hasn't heard. I tell him that if he starts in the middle of a story about Pokémon, I don't have the knowledge to join in.

I let him know that if I am acting frustrated, it may be something to do with the rest of my day and not to do with him.

Drip-feeding a daily dose of what's happening and why have boosted his social skills no end.

My husband and I had a rare weekend away recently, to Italy. I noticed the proprietor of the hotel used some very effective techniques to grab your attention. He would say something like, 'You cannot open the windows in the bedroom at night, because of the mosquitos. But you can open the bathroom window. Why? Because I put up mosquito net.'

This 'Why?' acts like a flag in a conversation and it's very useful for autistic people. We don't learn by being told, we learn by being told *WHY*.

In junior school, when there were social difficulties, we'd draw little cartoons and Bobby would try to look at the context and match it to people's emotions. What might they be thinking and where are the clues? That is so hard for autistic people, but being shown how to observe a situation and practising it most definitely helps.

I don't believe in forcing eye contact, but I do believe that we can't expect autistic people to accurately read emotions if they're unable to do this. They have to be taught about other, subtler, signals.

I was lucky in that Bobby needed to be shown how to use eye contact, but it wasn't a problem for him once he grasped it. We worked on it with our first speech and language therapist who taught us not to give him the box of raisins he was reaching for until he made eye contact. These days I'd be hesitant about training a child in this way. If we don't know why they are avoiding eye contact, it can be distressing to force it. For some, information overload from our eyes is too painful to bear. For others, the confusion is just too uncomfortable.

For Bobby, however, it was just something that hadn't naturally occurred to him. Once he was taught eye contact at the age of three, reading emotions wasn't difficult for him. We did a lot of quizzes when he was little and found that he could identify emotions quite easily.

After we had done quite a lot of practice at looking for cues, Bobby would look at my face before he nagged for something. On one occasion, he said, 'Wait – don't tell me. You're tired and now is not a good time.' I was massively proud. He had learnt to read me. Not only the emotion itself, but what could be causing it.

This doesn't take a lot of therapy. All it takes is a little stream of explanations, a running commentary on daily life. Emotional subtitles if you like.

One of the other techniques I used to help Bobby develop a sense of other people's inner worlds was Tummy Bubbles.

Tummy Bubbles came about when I got bored of talking about Skylanders. Bobby was about eight at the time.

'Bobby, can we talk about something else?' I said.

'No, Mum, we can't. I have these Tummy Bubbles – they are Mario, Skylanders, Sonic, Minecraft and Pokémon. They go from my tummy to my head, they take it in turns. There ISN'T ANYTHING ELSE!'

Okay, interesting perspective. It occurred to me that we could use the notion of Tummy Bubbles to show Bobby how his experiences differed from everyone else's.

I explained that everyone has Tummy Bubbles of their own, but on different subjects. 'What do you think mine are, Bobby?'

'Duran Duran and A-ha?'

Embarrassing. Kind of accurate, but still embarrassing. Much as I like to follow modern music, I'm an 80s girl at heart.

I sent Bobby to school that week with a mission to find out what was in his friends' Tummy Bubbles by asking them questions.

He took on this mission with some enthusiasm. To help, I asked his friends if they would draw Bobby a picture of themselves, surrounded by bubbles containing the things they loved.

Being the sweet kids they were, they all obliged – and Bobby's cousins joined in. Pretty soon his bedroom walls were covered with drawings of dogs, guinea pigs, Hello Kitty, horses, dancing...every hobby you could think of. One day Bobby's new girlfriend came home with us (he had five of them at the time, who he tended to list in order of preference). In the back of the car, he asked her what her Tummy Bubbles were. Lo and behold, she liked Horrid Henry too! They had more in common than they had thought.

Tummy Bubbles became a triumph of discovery.

Some years later, as Bobby matured, his empathy skills really developed. I began to start loosening the reins on myself and not to be afraid of showing him when I felt a little vulnerable.

One evening, when he was 12, I was feeling down-hearted. Being middle-aged and having twins with autism, I'd let myself go a little and had put on a stone (see the first sentence in Chapter 13).

I was trying to lose the weight and I wasn't quite yet there.

'Bobby, you know how I comfort you? Well I need a bit of comfort because I'm just not getting to my target weight and yet I do try very hard.'

As usual, Bobby wasn't slow to add his own advice, in his own inimitable language style.

'Well what you need to do is just to resist yourself.'

'Yeh.'

'And give yourself a reward for resisting yourself.'

'Yeh that's good, Bobby.'

'What do you like? Apart from candy I mean!'

'Erm I like music, and hot baths and...'

'Well if you resist, I will brush your hair.'

That's it. Right there, that's why parenting autistic kids is so rewarding. In that one conversation, Bobby showed how hard he had been working to understand my inner feelings.

One myth that I'd like to destroy is that autistic people don't have empathy. If you find it hard to read someone's facial expression and then match it to context, it will appear as if you don't have empathy. Not being able to read a situation accurately is not the same as having an absence of feeling. Bobby and Alec both experience all the same feelings as others, but sometimes you need to show them how to join the dots in a situation.

As well as editing the magazine with me, Tori runs a specialist support agency for young children with autism. We were looking at a picture one day and we decided to do a little experiment. The picture was a cartoon of a stick figure looking sad. The top of his ice-cream was lying on the floor and there was a raincloud over his head, with rain pouring down from it.

We asked three people with autism who work at the office to interpret this picture. Tim, who works with us on *AuKids*, looked and said, 'Is that a chicken's beak?' He could interpret neither facial expression nor context and had mistaken the ice-cream for something quite different. Clues in the picture weren't helping him at all.

Another chap in the office who also has autism, looked at the picture and said, 'He's sad because it's raining.'

What the rest of us do is look at a facial expression first, then fill in the gaps around it. He had looked instead at the most obvious element of the picture – the raincloud – and drawn his conclusions from that.

Our third autistic volunteer looked at the picture and said, 'He's sad because he's dropped his ice-cream and the raincloud is symbolic of his sadness.' She had more skills in this area and knew what to look for.

To us it summed up how people's skills can vary tremendously according to how good they are at reading these clues.

In fact, many people with autism say they are EXTRA empathic, as they are so keenly aware of what's missing. They put a lot of effort into thinking about what others may be feeling. In fact, for some women with autism, this is their central and exhausting focus.

So, experiencing a feeling of sympathy is very different from the ability to express empathy at the right moment and for the right reason.

Before I go any further, I think it's worth saying that we parents can be great at encouraging our children to believe that we are indeed mind-readers. This is deeply unhelpful if you already lack Theory of Mind.

If you know a child so well that you don't give them choices because you can easily guess what they need, you encourage the assumption that what's in their head is INDEED in yours.

Look! You're a mind-reader! But how come you automatically know that they want peanut butter on toast, but can't guess that they have a headache?

What is wrong with you?!

By asking Alec lots of questions every day about what he wants to wear, what he wants to eat and what he would like to show me, he has developed Theory of Mind. He knows he has to tell me.

Alec used to wait for things to happen. Up until around the age of eight, he was entirely passive. He let the world come to him. And because he was cute, and we knew and loved him – and because it wasn't easy to communicate with him – we did a lot of mind-reading. I used picture cards a lot, but only when I couldn't guess the answer myself. I did the guessing and he just sat there looking cute.

Then, through conversations with Tori, I stopped doing that.

I learnt to give Alec choices even when I already knew what was in his head.

Sometimes, his choices surprised me. I think he varied them just because he could.

Without the ability to make demands of others around us, we remain helpless.

Remember that autistic people don't know what it's like to be 'neurotypical' or non-autistic.

You don't know what it's like to have autism either, but since you have Theory of Mind you're in a far better position to guess.

So, it's up to you to help them fill in the missing bits.

But not too much. I kind of like it that I get an unfiltered version of the world from Bobby and so do other people. With a world so sugar-coated in gloss and spin, so fake and so two-faced, it's amazingly refreshing to talk to people who don't have an agenda.

Problems only really arise when other people mistake lack of social understanding for lack of intelligence.

With autistic people, there is no mask, only authenticity. When you're talking to someone with autism, you have permission to be as direct as they are. They prefer it that way.

You have to admire this different way of being, even if it causes them – and us – some misunderstandings.

12 Rigid Thinking Can Bend

Helping kids to be more flexible

I believe anyone can conquer fear by doing the things he fears to do, providing he keeps on doing them until he gets a record of successful experiences behind him.

Eleanor Roosevelt

As well as the fact that as a toddler Bobby would lose his temper quite easily, we were struck by his non-compliance.

At first, he said, 'No,' by just pursing his lips together when a new food marched towards him on a spoon.

Then, when he could express it more clearly, it became a firm favourite.

'No, I don't want to go there.'

'No, I don't want to try that.'

Then there was my particular favourite: 'N-n-n-n-n-n-n-n-n-nooooooooo.'

I guess that's a no, then.

Life could have been quite small for us – and it was, for a while. As he grew, however, I learnt something powerful.

In autism, pretty much everything is linked to anxiety.

Rigidity of thought isn't obstinacy, it's caused by fear. Keeping things the same enables autistic people to remain emotionally secure.

When Bobby said no, what he really meant was:

- *I'm not sure.*

- *I'm frightened.*

- *I don't like change.*

- *I don't know enough to make a decision.*

- *What if I try and I don't like it?*

- *What if it makes me so upset I have a meltdown?*

He didn't, however, have the expressive language or a good enough grasp of his own feelings to explain this.

'No' is a certainty. We know what's going to happen when we say 'No.' It's a coping strategy.

As they get older, the fear of what may happen when they aren't emotionally secure – a meltdown – can be enough to stop autistic adults from venturing out altogether. The possibility of distress and rejection is just too much.

If practised daily, rigidity eventually becomes a trap. That trap ensnares not only the person themselves but also their entire family.

But it is possible to bend, and one of the things that I've learnt over the last ten years is that a secure, stable, predictable home life gives their speeding minds a chance to settle down. As you know, I'm no scientist, but what I've observed in my twins is that certainty and security at home seem to give their brains a touch more room to be flexible. A calm setting seems to take them out of survival mode and gives them a better chance of adventuring when outside home.

That's part of the reason I feel that adults keeping things calm (and reasonably predictable) is so important, but we'll get into that when we come to meltdowns (bet you can't wait for that one).

Despite having a calm background, Bobby's favourite word was still 'No' and I learnt to help him question this by interpreting the word's real meaning in each situation.

Most of the time, 'No' meant 'I'm not sure.'

I started to show Bobby that there was a way out.

What about we try this for ten minutes and if you don't like it, we will leave?

What about you try the tiniest bit of that food on the end of your tongue and if you don't like it, you don't have to have any more?

What about we just let that sit on your plate?

An exit strategy and taking the pressure right off worked wonders.

Trying something doesn't mean diving in at the deep end and once a child realises this, it can seem easier.

We stretched Bobby and Alec's experiences just one tiny step at a time. As the African proverb goes, 'No one tests the depth of the water with both feet.'

I became used to making a small opening in the doorway to something new, but I always showed Bobby the exit.

In this way, he learnt to tolerate new things.

The amazing thing was, we never did have to leave after five minutes. Just having the option was enough. After five minutes at a new place, Bobby usually declared, 'THIS IS THE BEST DAY OF MY LIFE!'

Gavin and I then exchanged heavenwards glances.

You may be wondering at this point how we managed combatting rigidity with Alec. We didn't have to. The guy who didn't talk may have enjoyed repetition but in his pick 'n' mix, rigidity didn't feature. It was only when he became older and more aware of his surroundings that he became more rigid. We learnt to address his non-verbal 'No' in much the same way, by thinking about the underlying feeling behind it – fear of the unknown.

New experiences are important in making our kids more flexible, as they can fill gaps where natural understanding is lacking. Experience creates confidence, bravery and good, solid evidence that it's not as bad as you think it might be.

If called upon to do so, we always honoured our promises to 'try it for only five minutes' or 'eat just three spoonfuls'. This built up trust, which is so important where fear plays a starring role.

I was amazed at the amount of times that Bobby finished a plateful of something after agreeing to the 'three spoonfuls' rule. 'Hmm, it's quite nice actually!'

I tried to avoid looking smug if this happened.

Once you get the ball rolling, it becomes easier to look back on previous successes and use them as examples.

'Do you remember how you weren't sure of trying that? And then you really loved it? Do you think this could be the same?'

I began to ask Bobby to score his initial fear of something new and then rate it again after he'd tried it. We'd discuss the difference and the feelings that accompanied those scores.

When Bobby was in his first year at primary school, he hated dressing up and would only agree to be on stage if his teaching assistant attached numbers to his costume. When he was a shepherd for the Christmas Nativity play, it just looked as if he took his job very seriously. Senior Shepherd.

At first, he was given no lines, then one or two and, by the end of primary school, he was the guy with the microphone signing off from everyone at the end.

Giving Bobby the option to leave made him more flexible. In a similar way, he doesn't always use his ear defenders – simply having them nearby calms him down.

We want to avoid meltdowns at all costs – and so do our kids. If this means backing out of a situation entirely, then they will do, unless we can give them a good alternative plan for what to do if things go wrong.

It took planning – the resourceful teaching assistant used to mark where Bobby should stand on the stage and everyone was instructed not to step on his mark. He could leave at any point. His trusty Pikachu accompanied him – Pikachu was non-negotiable. This included the time when the entire class played air guitar and, with Pikachu tucked tightly under his arm, Bobby's air guitar looked more like 'When I'm Cleaning Windows' on a banjo.

Every triumph led to another and then another.

During the summer when Bobby was ten, Bobby and his best friend Jahmahl, who isn't autistic, visited the CBBC children's TV studios in Manchester. When the children were given the option to do some presenting, Jahmahl's hand shot up and so Bobby's did, too.

As they settled behind the presenting desk and were shown how to read an autocue, I watched with more than a faint feeling of trepidation. Both looked scared. Bobby's rigid body language suggested 'OMG, I am on the brink of meltdown.'

By now, however, he had learnt calming self-talk and could control his own responses better. I had to trust him. Besides, just having his best friend next to him was usually enough to have a soothing effect. Jahmahl instinctively knew what to do if Bobby showed signs of distress. He was just born that way. Jahmahl's mum calls Bobby his 'brother from another mother'.

The countdown began and for a second it looked as if Bobby would bolt. Then they were 'live' (not really) and, like magic, they read the autocue as a team, with feeling and enthusiasm. The congratulatory look they gave each other afterwards was priceless. We have a photograph of Bobby with his hand on Jahmahl's shoulder, as if to say, 'Good job, mate!'

If he can tackle that, I thought, he can tackle anything. I told him as much.

These days Bobby can stand in front of a hall of new pupils and parents, presenting his own experiences of secondary school as a child with autism.

He has come so far, with a little confidence and a lot of escape routes.

'No' sometimes does mean no and we need to respect that. But we have learnt to look behind it, too.

The other strategy that I have found helps with rigidity of thought, is developing the idea of a Plan B.

Life isn't perfect. Things get in the way. But if we react with despair if things don't go perfectly, we're just reinforcing our kids' rigidity. So, we taught Bobby the concept of compromise.

Sorry our little darlings but we can't make the world perfectly predictable for you. What we can do instead is to help you negotiate an unpredictable world.

I'm not saying it's easy, but there are two ways of reacting to a situation. Take for instance, the fact that Bobby's Weetabix has run out and there is only one left in the packet instead of his usual two for breakfast.

Bobby will no doubt point this out in quite a rowdy way.

Of course, I don't want him to have a meltdown. I don't want him to be in distress all day. I understand his rigid thinking makes this difficult for him.

I know, I'll dash out in the car, go to the shops and get him some more Weetabix!

No, I bloody well won't.

I might have done in the past, but these days we've learnt to think through alternatives.

There is another way – teaching them what to do when things don't go according to plan.

In Bobby's grand scheme, Weetabix isn't that important. A shortage of Weetabix is therefore a great way to practise flexibility.

'What would be nearly as good?'

You might say, 'Oh my kid would never go for that, they'd just have an instant meltdown.'

They may not go for it in the early days. Handling meltdowns well and teaching them a calm response does eventually start to affect their own inner responses, though. Gently bending the least critical aspects of their lives is a great way to start.

How about if we take this one Weetabix and we just add more Cheerios than usual to it? That would work!

After years of practising flexible thinking, Bobby not only obliges these days but spontaneously thinks up his own Plan Bs when his favourite things run out. Disappointment doesn't come crashing down on him nearly as heavily as it used to.

When his friend was ill and couldn't make it to our house after school one day, Bobby said, 'Oh well, he will just have to come another day instead.'

This was the result of working at Plan Bs a heck of a lot over the years. Believe me, these disappointments used to lead to meltdowns (or at the very least, him making himself into a starfish shape on the floor). But a bit of maturity and learning goes a long way.

Whenever Bobby is flexible, we both make sure we congratulate him, applauding how well he's compromised. I feel it's good to show him that we know these things aren't easy.

Things aren't a disaster just because our autistic kids say they are and if we act according to their own reactions, then we reinforce some of their biggest problems.

This isn't to say that we shouldn't appreciate that rigid thinking is an inherent part of autism and that change is deeply challenging. I wouldn't for one second ridicule the need for sameness, which keeps them emotionally safe from harm.

We can, however, be instrumental in showing autistic people that there's more than one way of looking at the same thing.

Recently, Alec had a wobble when I had to change the journey home from school. It made me realise that going the same way each day was reinforcing his rigidity. After that, we became used to travelling one of two different ways. I'd always tell him which one first.

'Today we go the motorway, Alec.'

'Today we turn right, no motorway, Alec.'

So, stick to a predictable evening routine at home. Make that place safe and secure. Daily routines are important for a sense of security. It shouldn't feel as if we're all living in unpredictable madness. But the odd tiny shake-up really does help. So bend those little things in life – don't always have jam on bread. Don't always sit at the same table in a café. Choose things that matter less, and do a little mental stretching.

One book I found handy is Lauren Kerstein's *A Week of Switching, Shifting, and Stretching* (2014), but there are plenty of other good ones aimed at children.

What is behind this rigidity of thought? Why does it happen?

Rigidity of thought is one key aspect of autism that no one seems too keen on explaining. Sometimes people call it lack of imagination, sometimes lack of flexibility, sometimes repetitive behaviour. What is it really?

I'd like to repeat here what I said earlier in the book. If we can't explain autism even to ourselves in a simple way, how on earth are we going to explain it to the rest of the world?

Autism isn't simple. I know that. But surely in the basic definition of autism, we can find a term that most people can commonly use and understand?

As I mentioned in Chapter 2, in the *Diagnostic and Statistical Manual of Mental Disorders* (American Psychiatric Association 2013), the definition of autism has been updated and has two main categories now – social interaction (including language and social communication deficits) and repetitive or restrictive behaviours.

The category of repetitive or restrictive behaviours can be explained simply if you see it as the symptom of a root cause – lack of flexibility of thought.

Lack of flexibility is caused by autistic brains having lots of short-range connections and a lack of long-range ones. Good at seeing detail; poorer at generalising.

Pretend play means making a mental flip from *what is* to *what could be*. Where one thing represents another, a small leap of the imagination has been made aided by different parts of the brain talking to each other. Those little flips happen when we have flexibility of thought. It's like hopping from one train track to another.

It doesn't mean, by the way, that autistic people lack imagination. Pretend play is one element of imagination. New and original thinking is another, and they are not restricted in that area at all. Imagination in the pretend play sense is just the ability to take a different perspective.

When Bobby had his diagnostic test at the age of three, the paediatrician 'flew' a wooden block in the air and made aeroplane noises. Bobby looked at him as if he'd gone stark, raving bonkers. That was not an aeroplane. That was a piece of wood. He wasn't going to copy such obvious madness.

This is concrete, literal thinking. His mind can't make those big jumps but is very, very good at detail. The advantage of this type of thinking is that Bobby could quite easily nail a job looking for gaming glitches.

The ability to use our flexibility of thought to make a new situation bearable is something that provides us all with comfort, and we take it for granted.

When we are going to a new place, we subconsciously gather up all our mental paperwork on past experiences and compile it into a lovely report that we instantly take to head office – the brain. This informs us about how to tackle new situations.

This work, done in fractions of a second, takes long-range brain connections. It's not just memory, it's also relating one thing to another and being able to generalise.

In autism, those connections that give people the ability to compile and generalise don't work as effectively. As Peter Vermeulen puts it in his book *Autism as Context Blindness* (2012), it's as if the autistic brain is an orchestra without a conductor. Individual soloists are great but the orchestra doesn't work together very efficiently as a whole.

Without this ability, new things can seem frightening.

Much of the stress and anxiety that autistic people experience is caused by fear of change or of the unknown. Sticking to the tried and tested (repetition) is for them a survival tool – to compensate for lack of flexibility.

Hence, you hear the word 'No' a lot.

Lack of flexibility is easy enough to spot when you're living with an autistic person. Bobby found transition times really difficult and at first I was clueless about it. Why was moving on to another task such a problem?

Of course, I soon learnt those strategies most parents are taught – to give warnings before change. We would warn Bobby with a countdown, using words and fingers. We bought countdown timers and sand timers to help our son's understanding of elapsed time – visual countdowns like this work so much better than simply saying how many minutes there are to go.

Countdowns worked like magic on Bobby. With a lot of autism interventions, you don't see an instant result, but with this, it was clear that warnings were just what he needed.

They became second nature to Gavin and myself and now form part of our daily routine. We don't think about them. Before we go out, before bath, before bed, they get half-hour, 15-minute and five-minute warnings. It's a system sewn into the fabric of our day. That's the thing about living with autism. What feels strange at first just becomes automatic.

All of these strategies have made Bobby relax. With that background level of relaxation and calmness, his system isn't on constant red alert and he is far more flexible.

One last technique that helped with flexibility has been massive – but it wasn't intentional at first. In fact, we didn't realise it was making Bobby more flexible at the time.

It's humour.

A sense of humour when you have kids with autism is essential for staying sane. There have been times over the years when Gavin's sense of humour has stopped me from crying and made me laugh instead. If one of you is joking, it keeps a healthy sense of proportion on most things.

For instance, when Bobby was ten, he burst through the front door screaming and ran upstairs. A slightly weary looking Gavin explained that he had just told him his Nintendo 3DS had to go in for repair. 'That went well then,' I quipped and we were both able to smile. When the pressure is on one of us, the other will lighten the mood. Five minutes later Bobby was over it – his moods are like a flash flood – and I had sold him the concept that the 3DS was going on a summer holiday.

It's not just parents who need to have a sense of humour, though. Learning to get jokes (and to be able to laugh at yourself) for kids with autism is great exercise that increases flexibility of thought. In fact, it's possibly the best flexibility strategy I've come across. Of course, having a sense of humour doesn't half give you an advantage socially, too.

Humour is so essential in fact, that I may write a second book on it. That's if I ever recover from the first.

If you're autistic, your main source of fun will come from very direct humour, like slapstick, where the joke is clearly evident. For Alec, it's funny voices, farmyard impersonations and tickles. For Bobby, it's people shouting at each other in cartoons and it's goofs.

Yesterday, Bobby spent a happy half hour on the sofa watching goofs from a spectacular show at Disneyland. Wicked queens tripping up over their capes, magic carpets getting stuck in the air, one of Snow White's dwarves falling through a level of the showboat... I've got to admit, that was pretty funny (when I realised he wasn't hurt, obviously – the fact that Dopey fell onto Goofy made it all the funnier).

I loved watching these.

Once.

Not ten times.

The autistic brain doesn't get bored so easily.

When I think about my own sense of humour, sarcasm and exaggeration for comic effect play a major part. While sarcasm is saying the opposite of what you mean, exaggeration is also not the best form of humour for someone who processes language on one level and very literally.

Bobby made a muscle at tea time today and said, 'Do I look strong?'

'Yes, Mr Universe,' replied Gavin.

Aside from the fact that this is a cultural reference from 1975, this was also a subtle form of sarcasm. Bobby corrected him, 'Actually, I'm Mr Elley.'

Lots of our humour comes from the luxury of having flexibility of thought, rather than concrete thinking. It's hardly surprising that our autistic kids' brains can't jump through hoops enough to get it.

That doesn't mean they don't have a sense of humour, though. It's just more, er...how can I put it? Well, in primary school, a new boy joined in Year 5. Bobby made friends with him very quickly. 'I like Kevin,' he said.

'Oh, that's nice. Why do you like him?'

'He can make fart noises.'

That's what I mean.

Laborious it may be, but explaining more subtle jokes works wonders. I like to see our house as one big training ground for the Real World. We can explain things that wouldn't normally be clarified, we can rewind jokes and play them in slow motion and we can look at conversations again.

I think teaching Bobby sarcasm has got to be one of my proudest achievements in all this. I can't take full credit – Gavin uses sarcasm a lot, too.

We could have taken the view that Bobby didn't get sarcasm and that we should spare him by avoiding using it around him.

In real life, other kids don't avoid using a certain type of humour just because your kid doesn't get it. The real world rolls on unrelenting and unsympathetic to these kinds of difficulties.

I want the world to accept Bobby, of course, and feel that others should appreciate what having autism means. Nevertheless, I know he has to meet them half-way. I don't want him feeling uncomfortable or as if he never quite gets what's going on in a conversation.

At first, he didn't get sarcasm at all. He took it entirely literally and got confused.

Then I explained the basics. Sarcasm is when you say the opposite of what you mean, because it's funny, and you say it with a certain tone of voice (demonstrated).

Then I'd deliberately use sarcasm (I didn't find this hard) and say, 'What sort of humour was that, Bobby?' He'd think and then reply, 'Sarcasm?' He'd get a high five.

Then I'd start using it with only a hint ('Bobby – did I really mean that?' 'Er no, was it SARCASM?!').

During the next stage, Bobby started to spot sarcasm with no prompting at all and would say with some trepidation, 'Was that sarcasm?'

Now he's surer, he just says, 'Oh ha ha, sarcasm!'

He's even used it himself. I asked if I could have one or two of his jelly beans (which he never eats, he just looks at them) and I threw a handful into my mouth.

'Oh, stuff your face with my sweets, why don't you?'

I nearly choked on them I was so happy.

Gavin likes to personify inanimate objects; it's something he's always done for a laugh. He pretends to be the cuckoo in our cuckoo clock ('Why did you keep me locked up all this time – sob?'), or he impersonates the cat ('I've purred. Now give me the damn food').

On one occasion, Bobby was sitting in the back of the car when he noticed to his delight that the sun and moon were in the sky at the same time. Gavin started to impersonate both arguing with each other about whose turn it was.

Bobby giggled helplessly and prompted him.

Bobby: 'What does the sun say?'

Gavin: 'The sun says "Oi! Get lost! It's still my turn!"'

Bobby: 'Hahahaha. And what does the moon say?'

Gavin: 'The moon says "No, you get lost. It's night time now! Watch the time!"'

Bobby giggled some more and eventually he became a star in the sky trying to break up the fight.

Afterwards I thought, 'Woaaah, this little story has helped Bobby with Theory of Mind and flexibility!'

Because the things we were joking about were inanimate, we could imagine whatever we liked about what they were thinking. They weren't threatening. It became a long-standing joke and I think it taught Bobby a lot.

Helping Bobby to 'get' our humour, rather than to avoid it around him, has increased his ability to interact more than you could ever imagine.

I also use humour to overcome stressful situations, by helping him to look for the funny side in them.

When Bobby started secondary school, he wasn't used to Physical Education (PE). He used to do gardening at primary school and avoided team games. He became much more involved in his secondary school.

I knew, however, that the natural methods used by PE teachers the world over to round up children would be quite hard for Bobby, as he doesn't respond to orders very well.

I said to Bobby, 'PE teachers use commands at the beginning of each sentence, it's what they do. Run there! Jump here! Do that! Do this! Watch the ball! Whistle – peeeeeep!' Bobby laughed. I said, 'It was like that when I was at school too. How about you count the commands and come back and tell me how many you got?'

In doing that, and remembering our joke, Bobby forgot that the commands could be a little stressful.

Jokes have the power to deflect anything. They are solid gold armour. They are a key survival tool, for us and for our kids.

There should be training courses on this stuff.

I would run one, but I'm supposed to be writing a book.

13 A Stitch in Time Saves 9,000

Preventing meltdowns

Age eight, the night before the twins' birthday. Bobby's cousins sang Happy Birthday down the phone beautifully.

'Sorry. My birthday's tomorrow, actually.'

There's nothing like the aftermath of a meltdown to make you feel like eating five chocolate bars in a row.

Helping Bobby through them and learning how to stay calm has probably been the biggest lesson here in 'Real-Life Autism School', the one where the only teachers are the kids, and the kids can't always tell you what they mean.

We haven't busted a myth for some time, and I do so love smashing them to pieces, so let's start this chapter by driving an articulated lorry straight through one.

So-called 'challenging' behaviour is not part of autism.

'Challenging' behaviour is a response to two things:

- a challenging environment

- the inability to calm yourself when that challenge arises.

A challenging environment can mean anything – social stress, work pressure, crowds, noise, general sensory overload...anything that puts someone's system on red alert.

When Bobby was little, I think I was too busy preventing him from bashing his head against our front door to wonder why he took everything so badly.

Alec didn't take everything badly. Alec was an 'easy come, easy go' sort of chap.

They were both autistic, and one of them happened to have serious anger issues. That's how I saw it.

Then you get the supremely unhelpful people who like to say that meltdowns are just an autistic word for tantrums.

A tantrum is a non-autistic child's way of manipulating a parent to give them their way. In the autistic world, manipulation doesn't exist. You remember that Theory of Mind is the knowledge that what's in your head isn't the same as in mine? Well, lacking that knowledge, autistic kids can't manipulate others.

A child having a tantrum has real control over when it stops. A child having a meltdown is taken over by their body's response to stress.

> A child having a tantrum has real
> control over when it stops. A child
> having a meltdown is taken over
> by their body's response to stress.

This is really unpleasant for them – and tiring – but they have little control over it once it's underway.

So, a meltdown is the body's unstoppable reaction to physical or emotional overload.

Anyone who wants to judge you for your child's meltdown should shut up immediately. A quick way of dealing with them is to say, 'Shut up immediately.' A politer way of dealing with them is to say, 'This child is experiencing an overload to their nervous system; it is to do with their autism and both he and I would appreciate some space and some quiet.'

Or, just ignore them. See earlier chapters and file under 'Who cares what everyone else thinks?'

Not all autistic people have meltdowns. Alec doesn't have them. He does find change stressful, but he copes with it by going into himself more (which is sometimes termed a 'shutdown'). If things get too much, he'll find something to twiddle repeatedly. Focusing on that enables him to shut out the rest of the world.

Our friend Tim does this too, in fact his senses literally shut down during highly stressful episodes. His vision blackens and his hearing goes dim. He becomes highly disorientated as his body goes into survival mode.

Meltdowns are quite often a reaction to a build-up of emotion caused by 'keeping it all together' and, because of this, parents of mainstream children often report that their kids manage at school only to cause havoc at home time. They pay a heavy price for experiencing the pressure to fit in.

I learnt to understand meltdowns through experience, not by being told anything about them. When they first happened, I didn't connect them with autism at all.

It only would have taken a few sentences for someone to explain meltdowns properly to me, which is what I'm going to do for you now. Well, someone's got to.

Because of the less adaptable thinking we described in the last chapter, autistic people respond to change and pressure badly.

Also, their idea of change and pressure is totally different to ours.

Basically, it takes less to set them off and much longer for them to calm down.

They also have trouble identifying what they're feeling accurately and so they can't instinctively activate strategies to cope.

Hence – meltdown. Cue blue sirens and a child running around the house like a party balloon that's just been released.

When we talk about autism at conferences, Tori and I illustrate by bringing on to stage two bottles.

Autistic minds, we tell our audience, are like lemonade, non-autistic ones like water.

Fizzy drinks always have a high level of activity going on and if you shake them up, they explode.

In the background, the autistic brain is always busy. There is always a level of fizz. So, when shaken up, it doesn't take much to cause an explosion.

In our demonstration, it usually helps if we've managed to keep the lid on the lemonade properly. In one case, this didn't go so well. By now you'll know how clumsy I am. Enough said.

We then turn to the water and we shake that up a bit, too. The non-autistic brain gets agitated and goes bubbly for a while but calms down very quickly.

Over to the lemonade, and it's still fizzing for a long time after being shaken.

Being innately 'fizzy' and lacking self-regulation is a combination that renders a young autistic child quite powerless.

What we have here is a person whose brain fires off rapidly when under stress AND is also lacking the ability to calm themselves down after that happens.

The first thing that we can do to help is to make conditions tolerable enough to prevent too much fizz.

You can do this by creating a calm environment at home and ensuring Small Fizz always has a quiet space to retreat to.

You can also do this by adequately preparing a child for change. When we talk about our 'ingredients for success' at conferences, Tori and I have a slide called 'Prepare, Prepare, Prepare'.

If something is going to change in Bobby or Alec's world, I write a Social Story™. Social Stories™ were invented by Carol Gray and follow a set pattern. They are designed to prepare children for a new situation in a non-threatening way by taking a situation from a child's perspective and reinforcing the positives.

There are plenty of books out there on how to write a Social Story™, or you can join *AuKids* magazine and look up Issue 15 on our online archive (ahem). There are also Social Story courses for parents, which is how I learnt to do them. *My Social Stories Book* by Carol Gray (2001), the inventor of Social Stories™, is a great one, though.

Lots of warning about change as well as photographs and symbols (which are easier to process than verbal language) can really settle a fizzy brain.

As I mentioned in Chapter 8 about communicating with Alec, a lot of my daily work is down to grabbing photographs and symbols that carry meaning for him. He has become used to this process and knows that when a sheet of paper with photos is waved under his nose, change is imminent.

Countdown timers are also a favourite of mine. You can buy Time Timers from special needs stores or you can use a Time Timer app. What works so well is that they provide a visual countdown. Not only does this make the abstract notion of time into a concrete idea, it also means that you've got an impartial referee. Hey, it's not me telling you it's time to pack up, it's your Time Timer. For the first seven years of Bobby's life, a Time Timer was my soulmate.

If you want a good book on these kinds of strategies, you could do a lot worse than Adele Devine's book *Colour Coding for Learners with Autism* (2014).

So, on to the second strategy for preventing meltdowns. Well, you'll love this one.

It's to stay calm at all costs.

Ha, ha, ha.

Hey, I'm not trying to kid you it's easy. Sometimes on the inside I'm sizzling with luminous rage, but I've learnt to ensure that my voice doesn't show it.

Quite simply, I adopted for myself a little rule. You can have a strict voice and you can have an 'I mean business voice' but never shout. Not unless you want a 24-hour meltdown.

I reckon you don't have to be perfect at this. No one is. But more than any single strategy I've used with my kids, keeping calm has had the most profound effect on them. More than that, it's made me feel absolutely in control.

> **But more than any single strategy I've used with my kids, keeping calm has had the most profound effect on them. More than that, it's made me feel absolutely in control.**

Bobby has absorbed my calmness and over the years changed from the kid who bashed his head against a wall to the one who's saying, 'Mum, I think you look like you are about to lose your temper. I think you need to do some deep breathing.'

His moods can still travel from Nought to Volcanic in less than the speed of light. However, these moods are fewer and further between than they once were and last hardly any length of time at all.

In short, never underestimate the power of something as simple as speaking calmly. In fact, if I had to wave a magic wand and I could change one thing about all autism parents, it would be this – that no one shouted.

You may already have noticed that ambulance call operators don't tend to scream down the phone.

When you're in an emergency, you'd be surprised to hear, 'Oh my god, you have FALLEN DOWN THE STAIRS?! ARGGGH!'

They are trained NOT to do that because they know that the way that they speak to a person in an emergency has a great impact on that person's ability to stay calm, to function and to think clearly.

If you are facing a meltdown, you are in the middle of an emotional emergency, and believe me your best Ambulance Voice will work wonders.

Do you know how I learnt this?

Very simply, by doing it the wrong way. If I shouted back at Bobby when he was younger, his meltdown reached fever pitch and stayed that way for hours.

I was not born calm. If you must know, I naturally have a rather short fuse. At least I did have one, until the boys arrived. Practising being calm for so many years – even when I wasn't feeling it inside – has utterly changed me. These days, unless the world is genuinely coming to an end, I don't lose my temper.

If the world was indeed coming to an end, I doubt losing my temper would help much anyway.

When I sense Bobby's tension start to rise, I know that I need to speak slowly and calmly and to take the pressure off. Whatever we were going to do, we don't do it. We wait.

I pause to assess the situation. Has it gone past the point where I can carry on what I'd planned? If so, we quickly need to change plans.

It really doesn't matter if we are in a hurry. If I shout and rush him, it will take twice as long.

If he is having a meltdown and will be late for school, I call the school. I'd rather deliver him calm and late than early and in the sort of state that will stay with him for the rest of the day. They would rather this, too.

During his meltdowns, Bobby loses his ability to express himself. He gives me words of feeling rather than words of meaning. I put this down to the 'last in, first out' theory. Bobby's language was the last to appear and is the first to go under pressure.

When he gets agitated, all the pressures that he's ever felt, all the adult wishes that he has ever felt obliged to fulfil and all the woes caused by being different come tumbling down like a house of cards.

'I HAVE TO BAN ALL MY RITUALS! I HAVE TO GROW UP PERFECT! I AM GOING TO HAVE TO FIGHT THE ENTIRE ARMY!'

I used to try to soothe him by replying to all his wild statements, but now I avoid doing that and I just encourage him to breathe slowly. By the time he has reached boiling point, a logical conversation isn't possible.

Dr Heather MacKenzie introduced me to the idea of teaching Bobby to breathe slowly and to practise it when he is calm. It really does help you when in the eye of an emotional storm.

Teaching an autistic child to spot the signs that they are getting stressed can be really difficult.

Meltdowns don't usually happen in isolation, they are the response to a build-up of emotion, and if you can be taught to spot that build-up, then you can put an end to your own meltdown.

So, it was important to me that Bobby was in touch with what he found stressful, even before he learnt strategies to cope.

It was quite early on in primary school when we introduced the traffic light system for Bobby, encouraging him to point to the orange light symbol when he was starting to feel stressed. Later, the stages of emotion were indicated in more detail (see *The Incredible 5-Point Scale*, Dunn Buron and Curtis 2012).

Bobby hated loud noises and we found that having ear defenders close by, even if he didn't use them, was enough of a comfort to prevent a rise in emotional temperature and to help him cope better throughout the day.

We identified loud noise and crowds as a trigger, so he would go into the canteen five minutes early at lunchtime.

Having definite times throughout the day when he could recharge by playing on the computer (which is what Bobby finds most calming) was also important to him.

There seems to be a theory in some schools that when an autistic pupil is coping well, they should keep asking more of them until they break.

This is a very silly idea, designed to destroy a person's confidence.

If something is stressful, and an autistic person is doing well at it, quit while you're ahead and let the experience be a successful one.

Coping does come at a cost and they need to have pit stops in the day in which minimum demands are placed on them.

In secondary school, Bobby's teachers are dedicated to creating an environment that is unlikely to trigger meltdowns. They recognise that certain lessons are socially more demanding than others and try not to timetable two lessons together that have similar high demands.

If, despite all your best efforts, a meltdown does happen, a quiet environment is best for cooling down. Sometimes just time free from extra input is all it takes.

Bobby has some pictures of his favourite things at his work station at school. They flood his brain with endorphins and help to calm him in times of stress.

I keep Alec's favourite pictures in the car for him to look at if he gets stressed, too.

Various comforting sensory toys are useful, including Gripp balls (virtually indestructible according to toy tester Alec) and weighted cushions – anything that soothes the nervous system.

Using his specialisms can also distract Bobby from a potential meltdown.

On one occasion, we were late for holiday club and Alec was getting impatient. Bobby was getting ready with the sense of urgency of a snail at a sleepover. In short, all the ingredients for me to lose my cool.

So, what did I do? I shouted at Bobby to get ready. Knowing full well that a meltdown would follow, I shouted anyway.

Once in the car, I tried regaining composure by speaking calmly and encouraging Bobby to breathe deeply, but by this time I'd blown it. There were verbal missiles flying left, right and centre.

While Alec was happy that we were finally on our way, I had caused a small volcano to erupt on the back seat. I'd have to try my other technique – distraction.

'Bobby, I have some good news. But I don't know whether to tell you this, because I don't know if you're in the mood to hear it.'

'WHAT?' he shouted, as if I had just told him that Pikachu was to be adopted by a family in Japan. 'WHAT GOOD NEWS?!'

'Well… The Digital Kids Show is on at Event City in November and I've booked two tickets for you to go and see it.'

'Oh. Digital Kids Show?'

'Yes, they have YouTubers and really cool gadgets to try out, virtual reality and stuff…'

'Hey, that's cool. Sorry about the meltdown.'

That's it. It was over. It literally took two minutes to go from nuclear threat to total disarmament.

Flooding his brain with something that Bobby really liked had instantly soothed his over-reactive nervous system.

Taking the time to talk after a meltdown has helped Bobby to reflect on his triggers and responses.

We sit on his bed and I grab a toy. He knows the rule by now – when I'm holding the toy I speak, when he holds it he speaks. We don't interrupt each other.

This makes us both calmer – he knows he is being listened to, but he also knows he has to listen to me. We examine our misunderstandings and we make a plan together to avoid them happening again. Sometimes we write the plan down. We have got used to thinking about thinking, meta-cognitive processes or whatever they like to call it in psychological circles.

Bobby supplies his own answers.

'What do you think we could do differently next time so that this won't happen?'

'I don't know.'

'Well if you did know, what would it be?'

Works every time. This line is used by my favourite life coach Dr Phil McGraw (mentioned earlier) and it's really useful for kids.

If we're getting stuck, I might say. 'Hmmm, I've got an idea about what might work, but I'd like to know what you think of it.'

The final piece of the jigsaw has been helping Bobby to get a sense of perspective so that he doesn't catastrophise everything.

Because we don't want to upset them, we can end up colluding with our kids' dramatic version of events, and that does them no favours.

To distance yourself from a worry, it helps to score it out of ten and then to talk about the score. This has helped Bobby to form a sense of what is truly worthy of his distress. Most of the time he has no idea that the horror he has scored an eight out of ten is actually everyone else's idea of a one out of ten. His worry has been based on terribly inaccurate assumptions.

I was feeling particularly proactive one evening when I wrote down a series of scenarios that Bobby might worry about and I dotted them around the dining room table.

I drew numbers one to ten in front of him and asked him to put his worries in number order according to severity. Then we talked about the order.

This wasn't to get him to justify his thoughts but to make him aware that not all worries are worthy of the same degree of attention.

It was also to help him realise that different people perceived worries differently. What may seem a ten to him would be a one for me. Why was that? Because he'd assumed something terrible and I hadn't.

I like using numbers with Bobby; it's a concrete language that ensures we are talking about the same thing.

And pressure? Pressure is just a perception, and autistic kids need to be taught this. It was a real breakthrough when Bobby learnt that pressure wasn't something that happened to him from the outside but something that he perceived from the inside.

Dawn Huebner and Bonnie Matthews wrote two great books called *What to Do When You Worry Too Much* (2005) and *What to Do When Your Temper Flares* (2007). I'd highly recommend them; they've been great for us.

And now let's talk about you.

If you've managed to keep calm and cool while your child rants at you full blast for 20 minutes, then really you could chair the UN Peacekeeping Force. A standing ovation to you.

Sometimes, we'll deal with a meltdown early in the morning and then get on with the rest of the day without taking a moment to think that what we dealt with was an emotional SOS and that it has taken its toll.

I used to dive straight into another task after a difficult episode. Now I've started to recognise that, without being awfully big-headed, our family's most important resource is me.

I've had mornings where Bobby has had a meltdown (probably due to the pressure of rushing), continued it in the car and caused Alec to be stressed out, too. Alec has then gone for me in the car. I have arrived at Alec's school gates quite literally in tatters and on one occasion was given a cup of tea and sympathy by Alec's lovely deputy head as I sat there sobbing while another member of staff dabbed the scratches on my neck.

The boys usually see-saw, with one being good while the other is playing up. We used to joke that they'd have a morning meeting in their bedroom to decide whose turn it was to be annoying that day.

On this occasion, both set each other off. We've all had days like that.

I am starting to realise that recovery time is essential. I guard my own time closely. I may see a friend, I may go for a nap or take a bath, listen to my favourite music or drink a giant latte, but I consciously take time to recover.

I wish I'd done that earlier, instead of expecting myself to carry on with my blood pressure at ceiling height.

I've also become absolutely ruthless at cancelling appointments that aren't vital when I've had a difficult day.

So, just think to yourself. If a best friend had a day like the one that you've just had, what would you tell them? Would you tell them to carry on with their to-do list, their meetings, their housework?

If you've been dealing with an emotional emergency, you need to take a break.

By the way, my friend Tim has the answer to meltdowns. He says it's to move to the Shetland Islands where it's nice and quiet.

Unfortunately, remote Scottish islands tend to be a bit iffy when it comes to Wi-Fi.

And lack of broadband would most certainly cause a meltdown.

14 When You Stop, Independence Starts

Helping them to help themselves

Bobby, age 11: 'Thank you for my countdown it really helped. Only 365 days till my next birthday!'

The stork sent Alec to me, I am pretty sure, because I am a very impatient person.

In a previous life, my walking pace was swift, my purpose assured and if the post office queue was more than four people deep, I'd grind my teeth and turn around and do something else. The world seemed full of slowcoaches whose purpose was to impede my meteor-like swiftness.

I think the phrase to describe me may have been *highly strung*. And also, *a pain in the backside*.

Then Alec happened.

It is 7.45am and we really need to be out of the house by 8.15am.

There is GMT, Greenwich Mean Time and then there is AMT – Alec Mean Time.

In Alec Mean Time, there are four hours for every one of ours.

This means that getting ready for school in the morning can be about as easy as folding sheets in a sandstorm.

Deep breathing is required. Lots of it.

Part of the reason why deep breathing is important is because I'm not prepared to do everything for Alec. In fact, if I was, the whole process would be a lot quicker.

However, I've been taught more lovely jargon that prevents me from doing this. I've been taught about 'learned helplessness'.

Learned helplessness is what happens when you do too much for children with special needs and they lose the drive or the inclination to do anything for themselves.

Don't encourage learned helplessness, urges the side of my head that belongs to Perfect Autism Mum. 'Pull your trousers up, Alec,' I encourage, while he either fails to recognise the urgency in my voice or ignores it entirely.

Alec thinks about pulling his trousers up.

It takes a while for him to process your words, I tell myself. *Leave him for a bit*. If I tell him again, he has to process the sentence all over again.

Alec thinks about pulling his trousers up some more. He watches birds out of the window. He smiles and wiggles his head from side to side.

I look at my watch.

'Mum!' shouts Bobby. 'Can you help me with my tie, please?'

I switch my attention to Bobby. His shirt is neatly buttoned the wrong way and is not aligned at the bottom. I fix it, and his tie (sod learned helplessness, he's nearly there), and turn back to Alec. He is lolling back on the bed and the trousers thought has temporarily floated away.

'Alec! Pull your trousers up, please!'

Alec slowly gets to his feet, a bit like a drunk leaving a bar, and, smiling happily, he pulls his trousers up at the slowest possible pace you can imagine. Now imagine it a bit slower, and you're about there.

It's about now that I have a row with my two inner selves. Perfect Autism Mum disagrees with Impatient Mum.

Impatient Mum says, 'To heck with it, do it for him!'

Perfect Autism Mum argues, 'Then how will he learn? Do you still want to be helping him when he's 20?'

Impatient Mum retorts, 'You know what, right now I don't care,' shoves some socks on Alec and ushers him into the bathroom for teeth brushing, where Perfect Autism Mum hands Alec the toothbrush and gently asks him to start brushing.

Alec thinks about starting to brush his teeth and then gets a fit of the giggles.

There is nothing funny whatsoever, is there? Except maybe I am very funny right now. If you're on Alec Mean Time, you're in absolutely no hurry to get to anywhere and everyone else seems a bit unnecessarily tense. It's enough to give you a fit of the giggles and in doing so forget entirely how to brush your teeth.

Perfect Autism Mum takes Alec's elbow and waits for the slow brushing to occur. If Gavin asks me to move my car about now, he'll probably regret it. *Okay*, I tell myself. *This is a test of my patience. This is my punishment for being an impatient person for 33 years before Alec came along.*

He really seems to be enjoying this, though.

'Mum! Where's my homework diary?'

Bobby, like many boys his age, seems to have confused me for his personal manservant. For a start, I always used to be, so why not now?

Why not, by the way, is because Bobby is now capable of far more than he used to be. We are working at a different level of independence for him and most of our current focus falls under the umbrella of 'finding your own stuff'.

'It's where you left it last!' Oh god. I have turned into my mother. I can even hear her tone of voice. And now I understand completely what she was on about.

'I can't find it!'

Let me tell you that Bobby's observation skills when it comes to finding things aren't exactly perfect. If Bobby tells me he has lost his ear defenders and they are nowhere to be seen, before I alert the media I have a five-second hunt for them. I don't know if this is because Bobby lacks discrimination skills, that he is so keen on detail that he cannot scan the broader landscape. Or it could be that he can't be bothered.

Back to Alec. The phrases, 'Come on!', 'Hurry up!' and 'Get a move on!' are all a waste of vocabulary. They have no real meaning to him. It's not that he doesn't understand that you're basically cross because it's 8.15am and he's tackling the stairs on his behind at 0.01mph. He does understand it, but he doesn't understand why. There are no consequences for Alec for being late. The consequences are all absorbed by other people. So, what's the hurry?

There are two times of the day when most self-care takes place. One is first thing in the morning, when you have a deadline for school. The other is last thing in the evening, when you're a shattered wreck of a parent. Neither of these times are ideal, but autism happens in the real world and I figure that if I can do my best 70 per cent of the time then it's good enough.

When we're not getting ready for school, the fact that he DOES take time to stop and stare is really quite a good thing and a lesson in mindfulness.

In some ways, he makes me question why we're in such a hurry to ruin our lives by living it at such a rate that we can't deeply appreciate it. Yes, in my better moods, Alec is my Zen tutor.

But mostly, I just wish he'd hurry up and get his shoes on.

Alec doesn't have to live in the real world if he doesn't want to. As someone with profound learning disabilities, he is always around a support worker who takes on the job of executive functioning for him. Between myself, his teachers and his support workers, we cover not only all aspects of his care but his social diary, too.

He's cocooned in the cotton wool world of a special school where all the teachers smile like Disney characters. He is supported to reach independence milestones, but if he does mix in a mainstream environment, everyone will be consciously understanding of his obvious disabilities and duly accommodating.

Alec also has no concept of what he should be doing himself and what I should be doing for him. How does he know the difference between putting a belt on – something that I would help Bobby with – and putting jeans on, which

I expect him to do himself? My expectations are his only signal and so I have had to learn to make them clear for him.

You can say poor Alec all you like, but this is a comfy place to be if you have autism. He gets shopping outings at school. He gets bubble baths at home. Vibe-wise, his bedroom resembles a nightclub (albeit on a Monday night and with no bar). I may occasionally feel a twinge at the lack of academic credentials that Alec has, but Alec, let's be clear, doesn't give a stuff. And so it will always be, I imagine.

Bobby, to use a phrase that he really doesn't understand, is a different kettle of fish. He's on the border of two worlds and will be expected to cross that border frequently. It's a much harder job and puts him under far greater pressures. Since dealing with pressure is compromised in individuals with autism of course, his life is more challenging.

One of the things that people outside of the autism arena tend to find most confusing is the strange mix of ability and disability that seems part and parcel of autism. Unfortunately, this mixture works against those who are at times inconveniently termed 'high functioning'.

It's hard to understand why someone who may be top of their maths class can't locate the bread aisle in the supermarket.

In my talks about autism, I talk about it as a zig-zaggy line, with peaks and troughs. A person with autism may show ability in some areas and be struggling behind their peers in others. This, I think, is far more accurate than suggesting autism is like a diagonal line on a graph moving from low (can do very little) to high (nearly 'normal!'). Autism, as we said in Chapter 1, is a pick 'n' mix of different traits, not always disabling but sometimes surprisingly so.

When we hear about 'savants' (like Dustin Hoffman in the film *Rain Man*), we expect that an autistic person's exceptional talents in some areas will be balanced out by huge difficulties in others. That's what we've learnt and it seems to make sense for us that if you're very gifted you may have to pay for it in some other way.

What needs to be explained a little better is that it isn't just savants who have this imbalance.

So, take Bobby – he's top of the class when it comes to computer coding, but he can't locate biscuits in a small supermarket, forgets when he's run his bath and has a very badly tuned radar when it comes to spotting social subtleties.

When you're a parent and you want your child to be independent, you do kind of rely on the rest of the world to give them a bit of a break. But others can only do that if they fully understand what they're seeing.

And then there's the other guy. The dude for whom independence is a lifestyle choice, and one that he'd rather not entertain if someone else can manage it for him.

As a small child, Alec was what people who do 'professional autism' would call 'passive'. This means that he let the world come to him, didn't get particularly aggravated when he couldn't manage things on his own and would sit at the breakfast table for quite some time before hinting that you needed to put a bowl of cereal in front of him.

Over the last seven years, we've done a lot of work with Alec to help him communicate with us spontaneously. This involved removing the five-star hotel status at home and downgrading to a rubbish bed and breakfast.

Apparently, this is called 'sabotage'. You pretend you don't know what they want and then after a bit of an uncomfortable pause, they learn to tell you.

I call it bad service, but for autistic children this is very helpful.

Tori and I never liked the term 'sabotage' much. We felt it sounded like a cruel plot to make non-verbal children's lives miserable. I prefer to think of it as more like pressing the pause button on Impatient Mum. She needs to freeze frame for a couple of seconds, that's all.

You're not doing it to be mean, and you don't hold back when the child is upset, you just avoid leaping to the rescue every time you know they want something. I don't expect perfect communication in return. Just an expectant noise will do. It's something we can build on.

At first, I was really uncomfortable with the whole sabotage thing. It took Alec a while to learn that I wasn't reading his mind any more.

Gradually, he started to communicate spontaneously, handing me the TV remote and vocalising, or passing me a packet of sweets and attempting to say the word 'open' when I played dumb. It really worked.

Playing dumb is actually quite fun when you get used to it.

I remember the first time I realised that Alec had got the idea. At the time, clambering up the stairs was quite a lengthy process for him, but he managed it with a bunch of bananas to tell me that he wanted one. I was overjoyed that he'd realised I couldn't guess.

Once this started to happen, I learnt something brand new. If you pause, then you help autistic kids to think for themselves. If they start to think, then they start to realise they have opinions all of their own. They begin to be less passive and it promotes their sense of self.

For a long time, Alec just felt like an extension of myself. I saw it that way, and he did too. He was entirely dependent on me, and I smothered him with affection, tending to his every need before he'd even thought of it himself. I did this partly because he was non-verbal and partly because the accident had left me hopelessly over-protective.

Then we saw a talk by Dr Heather MacKenzie and were so impressed that we hosted her the following year to speak on behalf of *AuKids*, raising cash for the magazine.

Dr MacKenzie, in her SPARK programme, which originated in Canada, spoke about asking autistic kids what they thought, rather than doing everything for them.

Thinking for yourself is a part of executive processing that may be disrupted with autism. Heather pointed out that where kids lack the ability to make decisions, parents and carers become used to *being* the executive processing part of their brain. We do those jobs for them.

She talked about helping children to think for themselves by gently throwing questions back at them and allowing them time to reflect.

When she said this, lightbulbs went off in my head. In every talk, I filter what I'm hearing for either Bobby or Alec's benefit. Here, I could see the wisdom was relevant to both.

The PACT therapy and helping them think for themselves have been the two most important influences on my parenting style.

Tori and I discussed this in relation to Alec. 'What do you decide for him that he could decide for himself?' she asked. The list was endless. I thought for him. I had become the guy's brain. No wonder I was so exhausted.

Alec's symbols book (he uses PECS) was already being used at home. I had been quite careful to duplicate any methods of communication they were using at school to the home environment. After all, you don't suddenly shut up when you get through the front door of your home, do you?

But I now started to ask Alec questions all the time and that's when we started to make the fist choices I told you about in Chapter 8. He would choose the cereal he wanted, the dessert if there was a choice, which top he preferred and what he wanted to do. He started to learn the power of choosing for himself and seemed to enjoy being asked.

I realised that until then I had unintentionally been treating him like a dimwit – he didn't have language but he did have thoughts – he just needed to learn to use them. I didn't know he had thoughts because I hadn't given him the chance to develop them.

I suppose it's a bit like me not having an opinion on which mortgage we should have, because my husband has already worked that out. If I had to, I would form opinions myself, but I don't and his decisions have enabled me to be lazy. This would be unhealthy were it to happen for every decision, and fortunately it doesn't.

But it did with Alec. To think on his behalf was a loving thing, but not helpful.

When I started to give Alec choices, he became less passive and his decision-making became steadily more bold and reliable.

It did still rely on me being a mind-reader, because the symbols that we have available are Alec's favourite things (updated as often as I can possibly be bothered). However, what he decided to tell us and when was up to him.

Alec is still non-verbal but there is an unmistakable difference between Alec aged seven and Alec at 13. Now he tells me that he wants to go trampolining, that he wants peanut butter on his toast, that he'd prefer Weetabix today, that he would like this episode of Thomas the Tank Engine, that the batteries have run out on this game and please can you swing me higher... I need help with this train track, I'd like a shower, not a bath... In short, Alec now has communication.

He now knows what he wants – and he knows how to get it.

If there's one thing I've needed to be reminded, it's to keep checking what my kids are capable of. Left to my own devices, I tend to get stuck in a routine. It's usually Tori who will tactfully point out that I am doing something for Bobby that he is quite capable of doing for himself.

Do they need help or am I doing it this way because I've always done it? Now Bobby is so much better at doing things for himself, I realise that his independence skills are a bit random. For instance, I expect him to pour his own juice at the table but not to put his plate in the dishwasher, which is probably less difficult.

Neither of my kids indicate that they want to do things themselves. It's therefore up to me to constantly think, 'Hold on – am I doing the five-star hotel treatment here?'

There is no red carpet and room service here these days. Oh yes, it's a very poor hotel indeed.

15 You Can Build High Walls with Scaffolding

Learning independence at school

Bobby age seven, when borrowing a Game Boy: 'Is it from the Victorians?'

I was chatting to a friend of mine the other day over a coffee – she's also a mother of children with autism. I said that looking back, I could hardly believe how little advice I was given about parenting Bobby and Alec.

I remember being told to use my hand to count down the minutes left before an activity finished. I remember being told that 'transition times are difficult'. Yet no one told me why I had to do it.

If only someone had taken my hand and told me two very simple facts, I think I would have learnt a lot faster.

The simple facts are these: autistic people find it hard to think in abstract terms and autistic people tend to be

The simple facts are these: autistic people find it hard to think in abstract terms and autistic people tend to be visual thinkers. Anything that isn't certain or that's open to interpretation is abstract. Nail it down!

visual thinkers. Anything that isn't certain or that's open to interpretation is abstract. Nail it down!

If something is going to take half an hour, use a Time Timer to show what half an hour looks like. Give warnings every ten minutes to help make that information more solid.

Rather than vague instructions, give simple and specific instructions. Give them the instruction, backed up by the reason why it's necessary. Don't assume it's obvious.

Having used a Time Timer for a number of years and become used to counting down with my fingers, when I attended Dr Heather MacKenzie's course she made me realise how a lot of schoolwork can be difficult for autistic kids because they are asked to complete a task in a vague way and do not have the planning skills to work through a job systematically. That is something we can teach them by asking them to look for clues about what needs to be done.

It was at that point that I started to ask Bobby about his understanding of a task. I started to learn what was going on in his head when he was set a piece of homework. Very often, his interpretation of what was required was very different to mine. How many minutes would be reasonable to spend on this? How much writing should he do to complete it? He didn't really have an idea.

All of these things are abstract.

I learnt to pin everything down and communicate extremely precisely. I also learnt to ask Bobby questions to check whether we were on the same wavelength.

I noticed that he panicked whenever he was given homework. It was as if the pressure was totally overwhelming. Well it would be, if you've no idea what is expected of you.

If you're asked to build a tower and you're imagining the Eiffel one, you're going to be daunted.

Of course, I knew that autistic kids felt easily pressurised, so this 'fuss' as his teaching assistant called it in somewhat of an understatement (each mention of the word 'homework' caused a small tornado) was unsurprising.

What helped me to help Bobby, though, was to see things from his viewpoint. I realised that Bobby thought of homework as a mountain, with more height continuously being added, and he had no idea how to tackle it.

He had the brainpower but not the executive skills – the mental scaffolding – to help him to plan.

Myself and Bobby's primary school teaching assistant noticed that he had the same kinds of problem during the day. He didn't always understand what was being asked of him.

I made a table. For each piece of work, I described what 'not enough effort' would look like (sad emoticon), as well as what 'good enough' would look like (straight-face emoticon) and finally what would be 'even better than good enough' (smiley emoticon).

For instance, if he was asked to do a piece of research on an author, 'Not good enough' would be cutting and pasting a paragraph from Wikipedia (something he was getting pretty good at doing). 'Good enough' would be finding a few different pieces of information from different websites and repeating it in his own words. 'Extra good' would be illustrating it with a photograph of the author and writing more than two paragraphs in less than 18-point font size, which was his trick for taking up an entire page with no work whatsoever.

Bobby did very well because of this. In primary school, he had difficulties dreaming up new stories, but once given an outline telling him to think of a character and a situation, he fared much better.

Once I'd realised this, I was able to convey to teachers that they needed to give definite expectations and a solid framework for him to work from.

Staying on task was also something that he found tricky. If Bobby wasn't interested in something, his mind wandered. His teaching assistant managed to keep him on track with many ingenious strategies.

He was given a definite number of things to do each day, with 'computer' pit stops as rewards. When Bobby had been good, he'd call himself a Special Good Boy or SGB for short. His teaching assistant spelled out the word 'special' during the day, with a letter gained for each piece of work completed. If they managed to spell out the word SPECIAL, he earned an SGB award. Three SGBs meant a prize from me. We worked together on this.

Constant communication with school helped us to reward Bobby in ways that were meaningful.

Once Bobby was in secondary school, there were extra homework expectations. To help him cope, I made him another homework guide. I'd highly recommend laminators; they make everything easy to wipe clean and don't cost much.

This table contained a list of his subjects, which he would tick if given homework. I would help him to fill in the date it was due in by and the number of days he had left to do it.

How did I come up with this? Very simply by analysing the way that I meet my own deadlines and constructing something solid based on it.

So, when given a deadline, we work backwards and become aware of the number of days left in which to do it. We work on the most urgent tasks first. Some children would be able to keep this information in their heads, or just work from a homework diary, but for Bobby it's important to have more obvious information.

His laminated table is pinned to the cupboard in front of his desk. He can see at a glance which homework needs doing first and this stops him from becoming overwhelmed by the 'mountain'.

I'm super delighted this month because he's started filling in the chart himself and, for the first time, completing his homework without me even having to ask if he has any.

These little pieces of scaffolding aren't much but they help kids to become self-sufficient.

It sure beats, 'HAVE YOU DONE YOUR HOMEWORK YET?' every night of the week.

When Tori heard that my mornings were just one long nag aimed at helping Bobby to get ready, she suggested that I do another chart – a tick chart showing all the tasks he had to complete in order to get ready before he could watch TV.

I thought this was a great idea and designed the chart around his favourite topic at the time – a weird cultish computer game called Five Nights at Freddy's. Bobby happily ticked all the boxes and before long he didn't need the chart anymore; he managed to get himself ready without the scaffolding.

When it comes to expectations at school, it took me a while to realise that although Bobby was now speaking fluently, he had huge gaps in understanding what was required of him. This was what caused him to be stressed.

Whenever he gets a little fretty, I ask him what he thinks is expected of him. I found out that his idea of being a perfect student and my idea of being a perfect student were two very different things indeed.

His idea of what defined a great student was to get 100 per cent in every test. He thought it was understanding everything that was said in class, getting things right first time and being interested in everything.

I had to point out that those assumptions weren't quite correct. Expectations were not that you'd do perfectly, but that you'd ask if you didn't understand, be willing to practise and try your best.

Once we were able to have those conversations, it meant that I could back off from helping Bobby with his homework. If he completed it in a totally different style than I'd expected, I resisted imposing my own way on him. This was Bobby's work, and if he wanted to write a

Titanic survivor's diary that started, 'Man, it was cold in that water,' then so be it.

Making abstracts into more concrete concepts also helps when it comes to understanding your own emotions. Back in the office, we noticed that Tim would sometimes arrive from his other job very stressed and upset, saying that he'd had a bad week. When we spoke about it to him in detail, it turned out that Tim's very bad week had actually been one unfortunate morning that had coloured his view of every day since.

Wondering how best to help Tim gain perspective, we invented a mood diary for him. We gave him a week-to-view diary and some stickers and told him to fill in each morning and afternoon with a happy, sad or confused face and a note of explanation.

By doing this, Tim was able to make sense of his feelings. He could see that although one morning felt bad, there were more smiley faces than sad ones in the week to view. There was solid evidence that things weren't as bad as all that.

Negative experiences weigh very heavily on autistic people, perhaps because they are experienced as so very stressful. Yet Tim's life in general was very positive. Filling in his mood diary, seeing it in 'black and white' as it were, helped him to see this in a very concrete way. He'd look at the happy faces and notes in his mood diary and it would make him feel in control and happy and would switch his focus.

With Bobby, I tried a similar thing. When he started secondary school, I knew he wouldn't want me to fire a lot of questions at him after school. There were five lessons in the day, so I asked him to tell me how many out of the five he had enjoyed. If there was one lesson he hadn't enjoyed at all, I'd say, 'So that was 80 per cent of the day that went really well? Okay, maybe we can talk about the 20 per cent later.'

It was a nice, mathematical way of getting things in perspective and helped him to compare certain days with others. This stopped him from catastrophising if things went a little wrong.

We're near the end of our journey now and there's probably a lot that I haven't covered. But I know you haven't much time and I hope that this has been a helpful shortcut to success for you.

There's only one message I want to leave you with, and that's to take any further lessons from the people who count.

The autistic ones.

16 Only Autistic People Have the Answers

Learning to listen

Ten-year-old Bobby's advice to readers: 'If your child has autism you'll just have to GET USED TO IT!'

I said there were 15 things you ought to know about autism, but every good record has a bonus track – and this is it.

You can go to conferences and you can read books like mine...you can listen to every radio and TV programme on this complex and fascinating subject we call autism. The one thing I've learnt over the last ten years is that your best information always comes from the person who lives with you. The one with autism.

It sounds obvious, but it's easy enough to ignore some important messages when you have a lot of alternative information that's glossy, assertive and easy to hear.

When Tim presents his talks on what it's like to have autism, they are the result of some really difficult conversations. He considers his responses and reactions and reflects on why he feels the way he does. He pauses for painful minutes as his mind jumps somersaults to articulate his thoughts.

He waits, he stutters, he physically reaches for the words in the air. I hold back from finishing his sentences. Waiting is something that I've learnt to do with autism. If you wait long enough, the words will come and when they do, they are describing something that you can't guess.

Tori taught me to help Bobby develop his descriptions. Instead of asking yet another question, I have learnt to repeat back to him what he just said.

Like, 'History was a bit difficult.'

'You found the history lesson difficult?'

'Yeh because...you know it was on something I didn't like.'

'Something you didn't like very much?'

Learning this counselling-speak means that our kids are in a better position to reveal themselves. The language is less demanding.

Autistic people aren't listened to enough. Maybe they sometimes speak in a monotone. Maybe they go off track, or can't articulately describe their sensations. But their voices are the only ones that truly count if we're to really understand autism. Don't wait for the most articulate autistic writers to tell you what you need to know. You have it around you; it's there for the taking.

With Bobby, information has not always come in a succinct and articulate package. He will mention something important one minute, then not want to talk about it the next. My learning comes in fits and starts, which is why it's been so important for me to keep the lines of communication open.

If you're chatting to your child every night, sooner or later, when the choice is theirs, they may come up with something eye-poppingly profound about the way they feel.

It won't be on a fancy PowerPoint slide or heading up the chapter to a book, so you may just miss it. To them, it may not be important at all. They may not have realised that this is something you don't know.

But sooner or later, they will say something that makes you say to yourself, 'Ahhhhhhh, so THAT'S why this is a problem for you!'

Sometimes pushy questions don't get to the bottom of things, but just making it clear that you're always available to listen can be more effective.

Yesterday, Bobby suddenly confessed that he'd been talking to his friends about his feelings. He had a huge smile on his face as he told me that he realised that they feel the same about some things as he does.

It was the first time that Bobby had properly talked about emotions to his peers, rather than to me or his dad.

If someone could have placed a banner on that moment, it would have said Here is the End of Childhood. Of course, he's still got so much to learn from his parents, but he is starting to learn from his peers too – and it's so important that eventually he feels independent enough to replace us in some key areas.

As for Alec, I've learnt to listen to him too, by watching. His focus tells me what I need to know. He is making himself heard in the best way he can, and we can't afford to be lazy, we have to always ensure that he has the means to do this. It's his right to be heard. We feel now that he understands us and we understand him. Well, it's as good as it's going to get.

One thing I've learnt about autism is that I'll always be an owl. You never stop learning and there are new discoveries about autism all the time. It helps to keep pace with these for my job, but I always bear in mind my pick 'n' mix situation and focus on our own needs as a family, too. If it will half kill you to attend a conference all day, with the parking, the sandwiches and the overnight stay, it can be just as good to buy a book by the speaker who has captured your curiosity. Please don't be such an owl that there is no room for anything else in your life.

As Bobby and Alec grow into young men, some difficulties recede into the background while new ones come to the fore…

Well, hello, puberty. I wasn't expecting you so soon. Come in, make yourself at home, trash my life, why don't you?

As Tori and I write *AuKids* magazine, we are continually reminding ourselves to rewind to the days when things weren't as clear for me as they are now. Some of this book has been hard for me to write because, believe me, after ten years, autism parenting becomes so second nature that you don't even realise you're doing it half the time.

Then someone who doesn't have an autistic child comes to visit and comments on your strategies. This is just life to you. My brother refers to it as Uber Parenting. It's parenting, with a cherry on top. A bit like the Autism Sundae Dessert.

I still have my moments when I wish the autism didn't get in the way of things, when I wish life was simpler, easier and less limiting.

But I do not wish to reinvent my own kids. A long time ago, I asked God (via the religious sentiment you suddenly develop when you want something badly) to grant me kids. I didn't exactly specify which type.

Bobby and Alec have taught me so much. Apart from the 15 things in this book, there's the little things like these:

- The scale of destruction caused by them making their own breakfast cereal always seems worse than it really is.

- You might think you're a big deal in this world but unless you can create a decent train track, you're nothing.

- Anything that appears to be unbreakable obviously hasn't met Alec yet.

- If you want to get anything done, wait until someone else has your kids.

One major lesson I've learnt is to surround myself with positive people who give me energy. I guard my time and my energy more closely than ever these days. I look after myself and if my mental health is taking a dip, I've learnt to ask for help, reassurance, a break…whatever it takes.

You don't need to struggle with autism or wish it wasn't. We aren't stood in the unlucky corner. We are living with autism, not an imperfect version of a normal life.

This IS a normal life. Own it, claim it, don't swap it – it's yours.

Life for me has become somewhat easier recently and if it's not as easy as other people's, well it's taught me to appreciate leisure, friends and family on a scale that I never had done before.

It's also highlighted some stuff about me that I never knew. That Gavin and I had enough strength in us to climb these mountains and still be smiling through the challenges has been a lovely thing to discover. But that strength has come from having great people on our side and not standing for those who couldn't or wouldn't help.

There are so many things I love about autism. Autistic passions give so much to the world. Autism is a world without pretence – people with autism ask not to be judged and in return they don't judge you back. There is a beauty in living with people who don't manipulate.

> This IS a normal life. Own it, claim it, don't swap it – it's yours.

Autism has brought me into contact with some of the loveliest, most genuine people I could ever hope to meet.

Autistic children aren't always rewarding. They take their time in trusting and communicating. Those people who work with them are the sort who give with no expectation of receiving in return. They have taught me such valuable lessons in what it means to be truly human.

Well, it's time for me to go as I'm starting to sound worthy all over again.

It's difficult handing this over to you. There's so much else that I want to say, but this is a start.

I hope you've enjoyed this book and it shores you up with the patience and energy you'll need to get the best out of your youngster. Be proud that you're the one to raise such a special person.

It's only fitting that I give someone with autism the final word on this.

Bobby has this message for parents of children with autism:

'Don't take it too hard and NEVER tantrum about it.'

And now, if you don't mind, I'm off to see which teenager wants to hang out with me the least.

Guide to Unusual
Idioms and Phrases

A pain in the backside Annoying.

A pain in the neck Annoying.

A ray of sunshine Something or someone that brings joy.

A rise in emotional temperature Getting upset.

A standing ovation to you Very well done to you.

A stitch in time saves nine Doing something early saves a lot of work later on.

A thin line to tread A very delicate situation to encounter.

A Time Timer was my soulmate A Time Timer was absolutely indispensable, like a friend to me.

A Top C that would shatter a window five miles away A very high scream.

Adrenalin junkie Someone who likes being a daredevil.

Ambulance Voice The tone of concern and sympathy used by ambulance call handlers.

An emotional SOS An emotional emergency.

Arrogant as heck I'm being really arrogant, here.

Autism circles Social groups involving those connected with autism.

Autistic mind as the holiday cottage from hell We shouldn't think of autistic mentality as something we don't want to empathise with or understand just because it's difficult.

Badly tuned radar Not aware of.

Bamboozle Confuse.

Become a keynote speaker on Duracell batteries when you didn't actually sign up for the Duracell conference in the first place When someone speaks about their special interest, in this case the example used is batteries, without thinking about whether someone else wanted to hear about the subject.

Biffing a teacher over the head with a frying pan A joke – I wouldn't seriously recommend anyone hitting anyone else over the head with a frying pan, but it just describes how parents sometimes feel when misunderstandings occur.

Bigger fish to fry More important things to think about.

Blown out of the water Completely dismissed.

Boils down to The basic point of this is…

Bored to tears Really very bored.

Brain freeze Neuralgia caused by eating something cold too fast.

Brick by brick Bit by bit.

Brother from another mother So close it's as if they are siblings.

Btw By the way (text-speak).

Busted a myth Destroyed a myth.

Buzzword Popular word used in the media at the moment.

Catch the vibe Your mood influences other people.

Caused a small tornado Caused distress and upset.

Climb these mountains Overcome these hurdles in life.

Cocooned in the cotton wool world Brought up in a very nurturing environment where nothing is allowed to harm them.

Colour in the blanks Understand the information that's missing.

Computer whizz Someone who is great with computers.

Couldn't give a monkey's I really couldn't care less.

Cue blue sirens This is a metaphor for saying an emergency is about to happen.

Cut me some slack Decrease your expectations of me.

Cut to the chase Get to the point.

Different kettle of fish Totally different situation.

Downgrading to a rubbish bed and breakfast Living conditions in which only the basics are done for you.

Drip-feeding Using the same idea again and again.

Driving an articulated lorry straight through one Really destroying the whole argument.

Eased off the reins Gave someone a little more freedom.

Easy come, easy go A relaxed attitude.

Fall into line Conform.

Fast-food language Quick and easy language.

Fewer and further between Less often.

Five-star hotel status Living conditions in which everything is done for you.

Floor-swallow-me-up feeling Severe embarrassment.

Foot off the pedal day Day where you don't focus on being productive at all.

Freeze frame Keep that moment in mind.

Get one over on To win at someone else's expense.

Gets a kick out of Enjoys very much.

He started to blossom He made wonderful progress.

Highly strung Very tense person.

His mind jumps somersaults He has to think about one situation and then something totally different and connect the two.

How very dare you This is just 'how dare you' but the phrase 'how very dare you' was made famous by the character Derek Fey on *The Catherine Tate Show*. He used it to express utter disdain.

I can't walk around Alec's head I can't know what Alec is thinking or experiencing for sure.

I was torn I didn't know which way to turn.

I'd played a lot of negative tapes in my head I'd told myself negative things again and again.

If life gives you lemons, make lemonade Make the best with what you have been given.

Impaired shmim-paired This is a Yiddish way of ridiculing the word 'impaired' – really it means 'Impaired? Hardly!'

In the eye of an emotional storm In the middle of dealing with a meltdown.

In the happy corner/in the sad corner An assumption made that someone stays in one mood all the time because of their life situation and that people who are 'disabled' and their families are always miserable.

In the same boat In the same situation.

Is for saps Is for weaklings.

It doesn't take a minute It doesn't take long.

Lightbulbs went off in my head Ideas came into my mind.

Little person Child.

Lollops Walks in a lopsided way.

Meltdown Extreme distress leading to a large and lengthy outburst.

Mental folder A poetic term for storing something in your memory.

Mental note Try to remember this in my head.

Mental scaffolding The ideas and thoughts that support you as you complete a task.

Missed a trick Missed an opportunity.

Nail it down Make it definite.

New information to be welcomed to headquarters New information to be processed by the brain.

Nought to Volcanic Racing from calm to meltdown.

OMG Oh my god!

On a different pathway Making your way in life differently to others.

Other children are apples, ours are oranges We are talking about entirely different sorts of people.

Out of his comfort zone Outside of the experiences that keep him comfortable.

Part and parcel Part of.

Pendulum was going to swing Fate would take us in one direction or the other.

Pieces of scaffolding The ideas and thoughts that support you as you complete a task.

Playing dumb Pretending you don't know when you do.

Put him in a growbag He grows so fast it's as if he's a fast-growing plant that has been fed well.

Quite literally in tatters He ripped my jumper so as well as feeling 'in tatters' I had scratches, too.

Rain on his parade Disappoint him when he's excited.

Ramp up a gear Go to the next level up in your thinking.

Red carpet and room service I'm referring to top-quality parenting when everything is done for the child, just like being in a good hotel.

Rule of thumb A general, basic rule.

Run with it Take an idea and make it happen.

Second nature Comes easily.

Shake-up Swapping things around.

Shoulders up to nose-height in tense expectation Your shoulders were very tense.

Sick to the gills Really tired of…

Skating on thin ice In danger of getting someone really annoyed.

Slowcoaches Slow people.

Smokescreen Putting up barriers deliberately (usually verbally) so that other people don't understand you properly.

Stick out like a sore thumb Look different to everyone else.

Stopped me dead in my tracks Made me stop and think.

Sugar-coated in gloss and spin Describing the way that the media portrays things as better than they really are.

Swear to god I really mean this.

Swim among the cars on bicycles Describing the way that teenagers casually veer from left to right of the road on their bicycles.

Temporarily replaced with a glazed-looking fish Fish tend to have a glazed expression and I'm comparing this to how people's faces look when they are bored.

The longest ten minutes of my life It felt like a really long time.

The stork sent Alec to me The stork is a metaphor for having a baby.

They are solid gold armour They are a great emotional defence.

Thick-skinned Unable to let other people hurt you with their comments.

To be hit over the head with the news To have disappointing news brought to you swiftly and brutally.

To go from nuclear threat to total disarmament To go from a full-on meltdown to totally calm.

Touché You got me back, there.

Tower of myths A lot of myths.

Traffic light system A visual system whereby you can point to green to show you feel okay, to orange if you are starting to feel stressed and to red if you are approaching a meltdown.

Tripping up over their social shoelaces Making mistakes socially.

Two-faced Saying something to one person and something quite different to another – giving two versions of the same story in order to manipulate someone else's feelings.

Umpteen Loads.

Watching non-verbals like a hawk Watching body language very carefully.

We are talking a cheap date, here It doesn't cost much to take him out.

We turn their lives into a film starring Russell Crowe Referring to the Russell Crowe film *A Beautiful Mind* – or any film where the real life of an outsider is portrayed in a glamorous way. What I'm saying here is that it's only when great achievements are made that people tend to start to value those who are considered 'nerds'.

Whole different playing field It's an entirely different situation.

Why don't they twig? Why don't they get it?

World got bigger His ability to try new experiences grew.

You could chair the UN Peacekeeping Force As a parent if you're able to handle this, you would be good at international negotiations.

Your place or mine? Your house or my house? It's a metaphor for whose lifestyle we decide to call 'real' – neurotypical or autistic.

References

American Psychiatric Association (2013) *Diagnostic and Statistical Manual of Mental Disorders Fifth Edition (DSM-5)*. Washington, DC: American Psychiatric Publishing.

Aronson, T. (1997) *Princess Margaret: A Biography*. Washington, DC: Regnery Publishing.

Blackburn, R. (2011) 'Illogically Logical.' Talk at Benchill Community Centre, Wythenshawe.

Bogdashina, O. (2016) *Sensory Perceptual Issues in Autism and Asperger Syndrome, Second Edition*. London: Jessica Kingsley Publishers. (Original work published 2003.)

Caldwell, P. (2014a) 'The autism spectrum, challenging behaviour and sensory issues.' Talk hosted by Autism Oxford at the King's Centre, 25 January 2014.

Caldwell, P. (2014b) *The Anger Box*. Hove: Pavilion Publishing.

Caldwell, P. (2015) 'Unlocking the voice within.' *AuKids Issue 27*, Spring 2015, pp.10–11.

Devine, A. (2014) *Colour Coding for Learners with Autism*. London: Jessica Kingsley Publishers.

Dunn Buron, K. and Curtis, M. (2012) *The Incredible 5-Point Scale*. Kansas: AAPC Publishing. (Original work published 2003.)

Gore, K. and Sartre, J-.P. (1987) *Huis Clos*. London: Routledge.

Gray, C. (2001) *My Social Stories Book*. London: Jessica Kingsley Publishers.

Higashida, N. and Mitchell, D. (2014) *The Reason I Jump: One Boy's Voice from the Silence of Autism*. London: Sceptre.

Huebner, D. and Matthews, B. (2005) *What to Do When You Worry Too Much: A Kid's Guide to Overcoming Anxiety*. Washington, DC: Magination Press.

Huebner, D. and Matthews, B. (2007) *What to Do When Your Temper Flares: A Kid's Guide to Overcoming Problems with Anger*. Washington, DC: Magination Press.

Kerstein, L. (2014) *A Week of Switching, Shifting, and Stretching: How to Make My Thinking More Flexible*. Kansas: AAPC Publishing.

MacKenzie, M. and Preveza, A. (2015) *Self-Regulation in Everyday Life: A How-To Guide for Parents*. Winnipeg: Wired Fox Publications.

McGraw, P. (1999) *Life Strategies: Doing What Works, Doing What Matters*. New York: Hyperion Books.

Schneider, R. (2016) *Making Sense: A Guide to Sensory Issues*. Texas: Future Horizons.

Vermeulen, P. (2012) *Autism as Context Blindness*. Kansas: AAPC Publishing

Further Reading

Books

Cook O'Toole, J. (2015) *Sisterhood of the Spectrum: An Asperger Chick's Guide to Life*. London: Jessica Kingsley Publishers.

MacKenzie, M. (2013) *The Autistic Child's Guide: Presenting spark* (Self-regulation Program of Awareness and Resilience in Kids)*. Winnipeg: Wired Fox Publications.

Journal article

Pickles, A., Le Couteur, A., Leadbitter, K., Salomone, E. *et al.* (2016) 'Parent-mediated social communication therapy for young children with autism (PACT): long-term follow-up of a randomised controlled trial.' *The Lancet 388*, 10059, 2501–2509.

Online

Rudy, L. J. (2017) *Making Sense of the 3 Levels of Autism: What Are the Levels of Support Now Included in an Autism Diagnosis?* Accessed on 13/11/17 at www.verywell.com/what-are-the-three-levels-of-autism-260233.

Websites

Inclusive Choice: www.inclusivechoice.com

IPSEA: www.ipsea.org.uk

The National Autistic Society: www.autism.org.uk

PECS: www.pecs-unitedkingdom.com/pecs.php